Evidence

Fourth Edition

GW00373258

Routledge·Cavendish
Taylor & Francis Group

Fourth edition published 2007
by Routledge•Cavendish
2 Park Square, Milton Park, Abingdon, Oxon, OX14 4RN

Simultaneously published in the USA and Canada
by Routledge•Cavendish
270 Madison Ave, New York, NY 10016

*Routledge•Cavendish is an imprint of the Taylor & Francis Group,
an informa business*

© 2007 Routledge•Cavendish

First edition published by Cavendish Publishing 1998
Second edition published by Cavendish Publishing 2000
Third edition published by Cavendish Publishing 2004

Typeset in Helvetica by Florence Production Ltd, Stoodleigh, Devon
Printed and bound in the UK by Ashford Colour Press, Gosport

Library of Congress Cataloging in Publication Data
A catalog record for this book has been requested

ISBN10: 1–84568–037–5

ISBN13: 978-1-84568-037-4

Contents

1 Introduction

Basic concepts

Definition of 'evidence'

The meaning of 'evidence' depends to some extent on context, but the word is often used to refer to any matter of fact, the effect, tendency or design of which is to produce in the mind a persuasion of the existence or non-existence of some other matter of fact.

Relevance

'Relevance' refers to the relationship that exists between an item of evidence and a fact that has to be proved, which makes the matter requiring proof more or less probable. In the vast majority of cases, it is not the law that determines whether an item of evidence is relevant, but logic and general experience. General experience will often be expressed as a generalisation about the way things are in the world. The burden is on the party who tenders evidence to show its relevance; it is not for the party challenging relevance to show that the evidence in question is irrelevant (*R v Bracewell* (1978)). Relevance is important for the law of evidence because:

- irrelevant evidence is inadmissible (*R v Turner* (1975));
- the way in which an item of evidence is relevant may govern its admissibility (for example, hearsay, similar fact evidence).

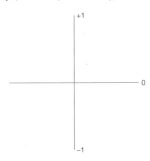

The probability or otherwise of what one party to litigation alleges can be expressed in the diagram above. The point +1 represents the mental condition of being certain that what the party alleges is true; –1 represents certainty that the allegation is untrue. Any item of evidence making it more or less likely that the allegation is true will have a place on the scale at some point between 0 and +1, or between 0 and –1, and will, in principle, be relevant at trial. Note that an item of evidence does not have to be conclusive to be relevant. Questions of relevance generally depend on the individual circumstances of each case (*R v Guney* (1998)). But a judge may decide that something that is relevant according to ordinary reasoning is not legally relevant. This may be the case, for example, where a judge wishes to avoid a proliferation of side issues that may confuse a jury or give rise to mere speculation (*Hollingham v Head* (1858); *R v Blastland* (1986)).

Weight

The 'weight' of an item of evidence refers to the extent to which that item makes a proposition more or less probable. In the diagram above, it is relevance that gets an item of evidence onto the scale in the first place, but it is weight that governs the position that it takes there. The 'weightier' the evidence, the nearer it will be to one or other extremity. Where the judicial function is split between a judge and a jury, questions of relevance are decided by the judge, and questions of weight by the jury. But a judge sometimes makes decisions about weight, for example, where the defence asks that an item of prosecution evidence be excluded on the ground that its prejudicial effect outweighs its probative value, or where the judge has to rule on the admissibility of an item of 'similar fact' evidence.

Although relevance and weight are distinct concepts, there is some connection between them, because the weight of an item of evidence may be affected by the form of the generalisation that is relied on to support its relevance. The bolder the generalisation, the weightier the evidence is likelier to be. But a bold generalisation is less likely than a cautious one to be true. So where X is charged with the murder of Y, and it can be proved that X quarrelled with Y shortly before the latter's death, the relevance and weight of the fact of the quarrel might be considered as follows:

Generalisation	Comment
(1) People who quarrel with others usually murder them	If true, the evidence is relevant and weighty. But this generalisation is certainly false, and, unless a more acceptable generalisation can be found, the evidence must be irrelevant
(2) Where a murder victim has quarrelled recently with someone, that person is more likely to be the culprit than someone who had not quarrelled recently with him	A little more plausible. If true, the evidence is relevant and fairly weighty
(3) Where a murder victim has recently had a quarrel with someone, that person may have had a motive for murder, and may be more likely to be the culprit than someone who had no motive	Probably an acceptable generalisation, so the evidence of the quarrel is relevant, but it is too weak to be anything more than of very slight weight

Admissibility

An item of evidence may be relevant and weighty, but inadmissible because of some rule of law. Where the judicial function is divided between a judge and a jury, decisions about admissibility are made by the judge.

Basic terminology

Best evidence rule

This was an old rule requiring that 'the best evidence must be given of which the nature of the thing is capable'. It did not require the greatest amount of evidence that could possibly be given of any fact. The object of the rule was to prevent the introduction of any evidence which, from the nature of the case, suggested that better evidence was in the possession of the party producing it. Thus, in *Chenie v Watson* (1797), oral evidence of the physical condition of certain objects was rejected because the objects themselves could have been produced in court. The rule is generally considered to have fallen into abeyance (*Garton v Hunter* (1969)).

Circumstantial evidence

This expression refers to evidence of a fact that is not itself a fact in issue (see below), but is a fact from which the existence or non-existence of a fact in issue can be inferred.

Direct evidence

Depending on the context, this expression may refer to evidence that is first hand rather than hearsay (see below), or to evidence of a fact in issue (see below) rather than circumstantial evidence (see above).

Documentary evidence

This expression refers to evidence of the contents of documents, which include anything in which information of any description is recorded (Sched 2, para 5(1) of the Criminal Justice Act 1988, as amended, and s 13 of the Civil Evidence Act 1995), and may therefore include such items as films, tapes and video recordings.

Facts in issue

In civil actions, this expression refers to those facts alleged in the statements of case, including facts necessary to establish defences that are either denied or not admitted by the other party. In criminal cases, the effect of a plea of 'not guilty' is to make everything that the substantive law makes material to the offence a fact in issue (*R v Sims* (1946)).

Hearsay

This is defined by s 212(2) of the Criminal Justice Act 2003 as: 'a statement, not made in oral evidence, that is relied on as evidence of a matter stated in it.'

Original evidence

Depending on context, this expression can refer to evidence that is first hand, in the sense that it does not come before the tribunal at second hand or in some other derivative way; alternatively, the expression can refer to evidence of words uttered by someone other than the testifying witness, where the object is not to prove the truth of the words uttered, but merely the fact that the utterance was made.

Real evidence

This expression refers to items of evidence that are presented to the senses of the tribunal and may be examined by it.

Testimony

'Testimonial evidence', or 'testimony', was traditionally defined as the sworn statements of witnesses in court. There are several difficulties with this definition today. First, not all statements in court are sworn. The evidence of children under 14, for example, cannot be given on oath in criminal trials. Secondly, evidence today can be given in certain circumstances by pre-recorded interviews and by video link. Thirdly, the old definition tended to obscure the fact that, in some civil proceedings, especially at pre-trial applications, the sworn statement of the witness was in writing. Such statements were called 'affidavits'. Under the more recent Civil Procedure Rules 1998, at pre-trial applications, written, unsworn witness statements are generally used instead and these now constitute the evidence on which the court will base its decision at that stage. Perhaps 'testimony' is ceasing to be a term that can be used with precision.

Voir dire

The *voir dire* is a trial within a trial, in which the court determines disputed facts that have to be established before certain items of evidence, such as a confession, can be admitted.

Functions of judge and jury

In jury trials, the judicial function is divided between the judge, whose decision on matters of law is (subject to a right of appeal) final, and the jury, who are in principle the sole judges of fact. Every summing up should contain a direction to the jury about these separate functions (*R v Jackson* (1992)). It is particularly important that the division of functions be made clear to the jury, because the law permits the trial judge to comment on the evidence in his summing up (*R v Sparrow* (1973)), although the judge should not go so far as to give his own views about whether or not a witness has told the truth (*R v Iroegbu* (1988)).

But note that a judge in a criminal trial may have to make rulings about facts, for example:

● where it is necessary to establish the existence of certain facts (such as those required to establish a witness' competence to testify, or the admissibility of a confession) before a particular witness' evidence, or a particular item of evidence, can be admitted;

- where the defence submits that there is no case to answer (*R v Galbraith* (1981));

- where evidence is said to be contaminated for the purposes of s 107 of the Criminal Justice Act 2003.

Although the judge's directions on the law are his responsibility, it has become increasingly common for judges to invite prosecution and defence advocates to address them on the content of those directions where there is room for more than one view about what they should be. Thus, in *R v Higgins* (1995), the Court of Appeal suggested that counsel has a duty to raise appropriate matters before closing speeches without waiting to be asked by the judge.

In *R v N* (1998), the Court of Appeal observed that it had frequently said that difficulties would be avoided, and cases conducted with clarity, if discussion took place between judge and counsel at the end of the evidence about points of law and, more particularly, about the points of evidence that had arisen. (Such discussion should, of course, be in open court, but in the absence of the jury.)

2 Competence and compellability

Competence has as its subject matter the persons *permitted* by law to give evidence. Compellability has as its subject matter the persons who may be *compelled* by law to give evidence. The basic rule is that all persons are competent and compellable to give evidence (*Ex p Fernandez* (1861)). Note also that the spouses of parties to civil actions are compellable on behalf of any party to the action (s 1 of the Evidence Amendment Act 1853). There are special rules for four types of witnesses.

Defendants in criminal cases

All defendants are competent, but not compellable, witnesses in their own defence, or in the defence of a co-accused (s 1 of the Criminal Evidence Act 1898).

An accused person is incompetent as a witness for the prosecution (s 53(4) of the Youth Justice and Criminal Evidence Act 1999 (YJCEA)). Where two or more persons are charged and the prosecution wants to use the evidence of one against the other(s), it is necessary to separate that person from his companions so that he ceases to be their co-accused. This will usually be done by:

- discontinuing proceedings against the potential witness;
- obtaining a plea of guilty from the potential witness before trial of his companions.

Where a defendant gives evidence at his own trial, he must do so on oath or affirmation and will be liable to cross-examination (s 72 of the Criminal Justice Act 1972). His testimony will be evidence at the trial *for all purposes*. Thus, he may incriminate himself in the witness box, and anything he says there may be used as evidence against any co-defendant (*R v Rudd* (1948)). Counsel for the prosecution is entitled to cross-examine with a view to incriminating him or any co-defendant (*R v Paul* (1920)). He may also be cross-examined on behalf of any co-defendant.

If a defendant fails to give evidence in his own defence (or, when giving evidence, refuses without good cause to answer any question), the court or jury, in determining whether he is guilty of the offence charged, may draw such inferences from that failure as appear proper (s 35 of the Criminal Justice and Public Order Act 1994). For this provision to apply, the defendant must:

- have pleaded not guilty (s 35(1));
- be physically and mentally fit to testify (s 35(1));
- be aware of the risks attached to silence (s 35(2)).

If the case is one where a jury would be entitled to draw an inference under s 35, the judge must direct them in his summing up that:

- the burden of proof remains on the prosecution;
- the defendant is entitled to remain silent;
- the jury must be satisfied there is a case to answer before drawing any inferences from silence;
- the jury cannot convict solely on an inference drawn from silence;
- no inference is to be drawn unless the jury are sure that there is no other reasonable explanation, consistent with innocence, to account for the defendant's silence.

(See *R v Cowan* (1997).)

Similarly, a defendant in a civil case who chooses not to testify runs the risk that his silence, in circumstances where he would be expected to answer, might convert slight evidence against him into proof (*Gibbs v Rea* (1998)).

Spouses of defendants in criminal cases

Section 53(1) of the YJCEA provides that, at every stage in criminal proceedings, all persons are (whatever their age) *competent* to give evidence. It follows that an accused's husband or wife (spouse) is always competent for the prosecution. The only possible exceptions to this would occur where the spouse failed to satisfy the requirements for competence contained in s 53(3), or where he or she was a defendant in the same proceedings. In that case, the spouse would be incompetent for the prosecution by virtue of s 53(4). It follows from the very wide terms of s 53(1) of the YJCEA that an accused's spouse will also be competent for the accused and for any co-accused.

By s 80(2) of the Police and Criminal Evidence Act 1984 (PACE), the accused's spouse is always compellable as a witness for the accused. But this provision is subject to s 80(4), which provides that no person who is charged in any proceedings shall be compellable under s 80 to give evidence in those proceedings. So, if a husband and wife are both charged in the same proceedings, the husband cannot compel the wife under s 80(2) to give evidence for him and she cannot compel him to give evidence for her.

The accused's spouse will, again subject to sub-s (4), be compellable for the prosecution and for her spouse's co-accused, but only in relation to offences that are 'specified' (s 80(2A)). In other words, the accused's spouse is compellable for a co-accused only in those circumstances where he or she would be compellable for the prosecution. The reason for this is that, since the prosecution cannot compel the spouse to give evidence in trials for offences that are not 'specified', it would be wrong for someone jointly charged with the accused to be able to do so because the result would be to give the prosecution an indirect advantage through the opportunity for cross-examination. For example, if the husband and a co-accused are charged with handling, the wife would not be a compellable witness for the prosecution because handling is not a 'specified' offence. But, if the co-defendant could compel the wife to give evidence in his defence, she could be cross-examined by the prosecution and during the course of that cross-examination she might have to provide answers that would support the case against her husband.

The 'specified' offences are set out in s 80(3) of PACE. They are offences where:

(a) the offence charged involves an assault on, or injury or a threat of injury to, the spouse of the accused or a person who was at the material time under the age of 16;

(b) the offence charged is a sexual offence alleged to have been committed in respect of a person who was at the material time under the age of 16;

(c) the offence charged consists of attempting or conspiring to commit either of the above, or being a secondary party to or inciting either of the above.

There is at least one problem with the interpretation of these provisions. It concerns what is referred to in sub-s (3)(a) as an offence that 'involves an assault on, or injury or a threat of injury to' the spouse of the accused or a person who was at the material time under the age of 16. The sub-section clearly covers an offence such as robbery where violence, or the threat of it, is an essential element of the offence. But it is unclear whether 'involves' covers an offence where this is not the case and the violence is only an incidental element. In *R v McAndrew-Bingham* (1998), the same wording in s 32(2)(a) of the Criminal Justice Act 1988 was given the broader interpretation, but this was in the context of a provision for the use of video and live link TV wherever a child witness was likely to be traumatised by confrontation with the accused. The court adopted a purposive construction, but it is by no means clear that a purposive construction of s 80(3) of PACE would have the same result.

In any proceedings, a person who has been, but is no longer, married to the accused shall be competent and compellable to give evidence as if that person and the accused had never been married (s 80(5)). Marriage persists until grant of decree absolute.

By s 80A of PACE, the failure of an accused's spouse to give evidence shall not be made the subject of any comment by the prosecution. The judge, and counsel for any co-accused, can comment. In *R v Naudeer* (1984), the Court of Appeal said that, save in exceptional circumstances, a judge should exercise a great deal of circumspection if he chooses to make any comment. (The reason for this is that, as with any other potential witness, there may have been some good reason why that person was not called.) But counsel for a co-accused may, presumably, comment as strongly as he thinks fit.

Children

Civil cases

A child may give sworn evidence if he can satisfy the test in *R v Hayes* (1977), that is, does the child understand:

- the solemnity of the occasion; and

- the special duty to tell the truth, over and above the ordinary social duty to do so?

If the child does not satisfy these conditions, he may be able to give evidence under s 96 of the Children Act 1989. By this section, a child (any person under 18: see s 105) who does not understand the nature of an oath may give unsworn evidence if:

- he understands that it is his duty to speak the truth; and

- he has sufficient understanding to justify his evidence being heard.

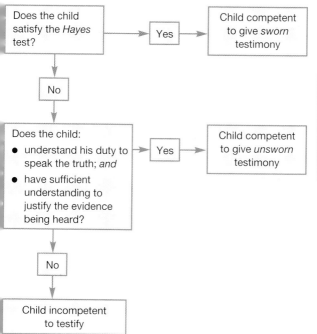

Summary

Criminal cases

The current law is contained in ss 53–57 of the YJCEA. The fundamental provision is contained in s 53(1): at every stage in criminal proceedings all persons are, *whatever their age*, competent to give evidence.

By sub-s (3), a person is not competent to give evidence if it appears to the court that he is not a person who is able to:

(a) understand questions put to him as a witness; and

(b) give answers to it which can be understood.

Any question as to whether a witness in criminal proceedings is competent may be raised by either a party to the proceedings or by the court of its own motion (that is, by the judge, even if none of the parties raises the issue). If such a question arises, the procedure set out in s 54 will be followed. It is for the party calling the witness to satisfy the court that, *on a balance of probabilities*, the witness is competent (s 54(2)). It should be noted that this civil standard applies to both the defence and prosecution. The issue must be determined in the absence of the jury, if there is one (s 54(4)). Expert evidence may be received on the question (s 54(5)). Any questioning of the witness, where the court considers that necessary, shall be conducted by the court in the presence of the parties (s 54(6)). In other words, the potential witness will not be submitted to examination and cross-examination by counsel, but may be questioned by the judge.

Assuming a child is competent to give evidence, will that child's evidence be sworn or unsworn? By s 55(2), no witness may be sworn unless:

(a) he has attained the age of 14; and

(b) he has a sufficient appreciation of the solemnity of the occasion and of the particular responsibility to tell the truth which is involved in taking an oath.

This is, in essence, the test applied in *R v Hayes* (1977), so belief in a divine sanction is unnecessary. However, witnesses aged 14 and over are likely to take the oath without further question because sub-s (3) provides that, if the witness is able to give intelligible testimony, he shall be presumed to have satisfied condition (b) if no evidence tending to show the contrary is adduced by any party. The effect of this is that children aged 14 and over will be treated as adults and no inquiry will be made into their capacity to take the oath unless an objection, supported by evidence, is made. If any question as to the satisfaction of either of the conditions in sub-s (2) arises, it is for the party wishing to have the witness sworn to satisfy the court that, *on a balance of probabilities*, those conditions are satisfied (s 55(4)). Again, the standard is the same for both the defence and prosecution, and the proceedings to determine the question will be conducted under the same rules as proceedings to determine competence (s 55(5)–(7)).

If a person is competent to give evidence, but fails to satisfy the tests for giving sworn evidence, his evidence may be given unsworn (s 56).

Persons of defective intellect

Here, also, a distinction is drawn between civil and criminal cases.

Civil cases

The old common law, formerly applicable to both criminal and civil cases, still applies.

Competence depends on the nature and severity of the disability, which may be investigated in open court before testimony is received. Expert evidence should be given on the *voir dire* to deal with the matter, but it should not normally be necessary to call the witness whose mental condition has given rise to the problem (*R v Barratt* (1996)).

The test to be applied is whether, despite any mental disability, the witness understands the nature of the oath in the light of the *Hayes* test (*R v Bellamy* (1985)).

Criminal cases

Sections 53–57 of the YJCEA constitute a code governing the competence and capacity to be sworn of all persons tendered as witnesses in criminal cases. Where a potential witness has a defective intellect, therefore, the tests to be applied and the procedure for determining them are the same as have already been described in relation to children. It follows that a person with defective intellect may be able to give evidence in criminal but not civil proceedings. In criminal proceedings, provided he satisfies the basic test for competence, he will be able to give evidence – if not sworn, then unsworn. In civil proceedings, an adult witness with defective intellect must be able to satisfy the *Hayes* test and be sworn; if he cannot do so, there is no provision enabling him to give unsworn evidence.

3 The course of testimony

Examination-in-chief

This is the first stage in the examination of a witness at trial and is conducted on behalf of the party who has called him. In civil actions in the High Court, a witness' pre-trial written statement may stand as the evidence-in-chief (r 32.5 of the Civil Procedure Rules 1998).

A witness will often be favourable to the cause of the party calling him. Because of this, two rules that are peculiar to examination-in-chief have developed: the rules against leading questions and against discrediting one's own witness.

Rule against leading questions

A leading question is one that suggests to the witness the answer that is wanted. An advocate may not generally ask leading questions of his own witness on matters that are in contention. This is because such a witness is thought likely to agree to suggestions made to him on behalf of a person to whom the witness is probably favourable.

A less usual, but always illegitimate, form of leading question is one that assumes that something has already been established by evidence when that is not the case. In *Curtis v Peek* (1864), the issue was whether a particular custom existed. The witness had not yet given evidence of that fact and it was held improper to ask whether certain conduct was in accordance with the custom, because that question assumed the custom to exist.

Rule against discrediting one's own witness

A witness called by a party should have been put forward on the basis that he is honest. If a witness' evidence unexpectedly turns out to be contrary to the interest of the party who has called him, the latter cannot repair the damage by trying to show that the witness is of bad character (*Wright v Beckett* (1834)). But the party who has called the witness may, in such a case, call other witnesses to contradict the damaging testimony (*Ewer v Ambrose* (1825)). He may also, in some circumstances, show that the witness has previously made a statement inconsistent with the testimony given (*Greenough v Eccles* (1859)).

Cross-examination

The objects of cross-examination are to complete and correct the story told by a witness in examination-in-chief. Because of this, the right to cross-examine can be exercised by anyone whose interests have been affected by the testimony. Thus, co-plaintiffs and co-defendants may cross-examine each other (*Lord v Colvin* (1855); *R v Hadwen* (1902)). For the same reason, the scope of cross-examination is not confined to those matters dealt with during evidence-in-chief, but extends to all relevant matters (*Berwick-upon-Tweed Corp v Murray* (1850)).

Because the witness that is cross-examined may be unfavourable to the party cross-examining, there is no reason for a rule against leading questions. Since the cross-examining party has not been responsible for bringing the witness before the court, he does not vouch for the witness' character, and so may discredit him by all the proper means at his disposal.

But evidence obtained by cross-examination must still be admissible under the ordinary rules of evidence. Thus, a defendant must not be cross-examined about evidence that is inadmissible in relation to the case against him, even though it may be admissible in relation to a co-defendant. In *R v Windass* (1989), it was held that a defendant should not have been asked questions in cross-examination about the contents of a co-defendant's diary that had been written without any contribution from him. And, in *R v Gray* (1998), it was held to be generally improper for the prosecution to cross-examine one defendant about the contents of a co-defendant's interview with the police.

Cross-examining the police on other cases

It was held in *R v Edwards* (1991) that police officers should not be asked about:

- untried allegations of perjury made against them, or about complaints not yet ruled on by the Police Complaints Authority;

- discreditable conduct by other officers, whether or not in the same squad.

However, an officer could be asked about a case involving a different defendant, in which the officer had given evidence and in which the defendant had been acquitted, *where that acquittal necessarily indicated that the jury had disbelieved the officer's testimony*. But, in the absence of any reasons for a jury's verdict, this is an impossible test to satisfy. In *R v Meads* (1996), the Court of Appeal apparently approved a prosecutor's concession that defence cross-examination was permissible where a previous acquittal merely 'pointed to' fabrication of evidence by a police officer. The law remains unsettled. See *R v Guney* (1998), where *Edwards* was treated as binding authority but *Meads* was not cited.

Cross-examination of complainants in sex cases

The credibility of a witness is a relevant fact in any case, because it is something that makes that witness' testimony about other relevant matters either more or less likely to be true. Cross-examination of a witness may be relevant either solely to credibility, or solely to an issue in the case, or to a mixture of both. For some centuries, moral character was regarded as relevant to credibility, and witnesses in any type of case could therefore be cross-examined about matters, including sexual habits that were thought to reflect on their morality, and so on their credibility. The position was no different where a complainant alleged rape or a similar offence.

The current law is contained in ss 41–43 of the Youth Justice and Criminal Evidence Act 1999 (YJCEA). Section 41(1) puts a significant restriction on the way the defence can conduct its case where the defendant is charged with what the Act calls a 'sexual offence'. This is defined in s 62 of the YJCEA and includes, among other offences, rape, indecent assault, unlawful sexual intercourse and any attempt to commit these offences.

The restriction imposed by s 41(1) is that, except with the leave of the court, no evidence may be adduced by the defence, nor any questions asked in cross-examination, 'about any sexual behaviour of the complainant'. 'Sexual behaviour' is defined in s 42(1)(c) as:

> . . . any sexual behaviour or other sexual experience, whether or not involving any accused or other person, but excluding (except in s 41(3)(c)(i) and (5)(a)) anything alleged to have taken place as part of the event which is the subject matter of the charge . . .

Thus, the YJCEA excludes questions about a complainant's previous sexual experience with the defendant as well as with others.

By s 41(2), the court may give leave to adduce evidence of the complainant's sexual behaviour, or to allow cross-examination about it if, and only if, it is satisfied of two matters: first, that either sub-s (3) or sub-s (5) applies; and, secondly, that a refusal of leave might have the result of rendering unsafe a conclusion of the trier of fact on any relevant issue in the case.

The expression 'any relevant issue in the case' is defined by s 42(1)(a) as 'any issue falling to be proved by the prosecution or defence in the trial of the accused'. In a rape trial, of course, the defence has no burden of proof, but this is not the case with all the sexual offences covered by the Act. See, for example, the offence created by s 128 of the Mental Health Act 1959, which makes it unlawful for a member of hospital staff to have sexual intercourse with a woman receiving treatment for mental disorder at that hospital.

The scope of sub-s (3)

This sub-section distinguishes between cases where the evidence or question in cross-examination relates to a relevant issue, but that issue is not one of consent, and those cases where the relevant issue *is* one of consent. The expression 'issue of consent' is defined in s 42(1)(b) as 'any issue whether the complainant in fact consented to the conduct constituting the offence with which the accused is charged (and accordingly does not include any issue as to the belief of the accused that the complainant so consented)'. So, if the defence is not that the complainant consented, but that the defendant *believed that she was consenting*, the sole test is whether the evidence or question relates to a relevant issue in the case and the restrictions imposed by s 41(3)(b) and (c) will not apply.

But the test of relevance where such a defence is put forward has been strictly applied. In *R v Barton* (1987), the defence to a rape charge was mistaken belief that the complainant had consented. The defendant wanted to call evidence of the complainant's sexual experiences with other men to establish the foundation for that belief, but the trial judge refused leave. The Court of Appeal upheld this decision and drew a distinction between belief that a woman *would consent if asked* and belief that a woman *is consenting* to a particular act of intercourse.

Sub-section 41(3) applies if the evidence or question in cross-examination relates to a relevant issue in the case *and either*:

(a) that issue is not an issue of consent; or

(b) it is an issue of consent, and the sexual behaviour of the complainant to which the evidence or question relates is alleged to have taken place at or about the same time as the event which is the subject matter of the charge; or

(c) it is an issue of consent and the sexual behaviour of the complainant is alleged to have been, in any respect, so similar –

(i) to any sexual behaviour of the complainant which the defendant alleges took place as part of the event which is the subject matter of the charge; or

(ii) to any other sexual behaviour of the complainant which the defendant alleges took place at or about the same time as that event,

that the similarity cannot reasonably be explained as a coincidence.

Sub-section (3)(b) allows the court to look, but only to a limited extent, at the context in which the event which is the subject matter of the charge is alleged to have taken place.

Sub-section (3)(c) allows the court to look at the sexual behaviour of the complainant on other occasions where that behaviour is so similar to the behaviour of the complainant on the occasion under investigation that the similarity cannot be explained as a coincidence. The behaviour may match either some element alleged by the defendant to have been part of the event that has led to the charge, or some feature of its surrounding circumstances within the limitations just described. It also appears to cover behaviour either before or after the alleged offence.

By s 41(4), no evidence or question shall be regarded as relating to a relevant issue in the case if it appears to the court to be reasonable to assume that the sole or main purpose of the defence is to impugn the credibility of the complainant as a witness. Of course, in one sense, evidence and questions about a complainant's sexual behaviour are bound to be designed to impugn the credibility of the complainant: the whole purpose of such questioning and evidence will be to create a reasonable doubt about whether the complainant is telling the truth when he or she says that sexual intercourse took place without consent. This can hardly be what the sub-section refers to. It presumably refers to the old common law rule, originally abolished for complainants in 'rape offences' under the Sexual

Offences (Amendment) Act 1976, that permitted evidence of immorality to be adduced to discredit generally what a witness said on oath.

Sub-section (5)

This exception to the general prohibition applies if the evidence or question relates to any evidence adduced *by the prosecution* about any sexual behaviour of the complainant. So, if during examination-in-chief the complainant states that she was a virgin before she was raped, the defence may cross-examine with the object of rebutting that assertion and call evidence to do so if need be.

Sub-section (6)

This provides that, for the purposes of sub-ss (3) and (5), the evidence that is permitted to be called must relate to specific instances of alleged sexual behaviour by the defendant.

Procedure

By s 43, an application for leave under s 41 shall be heard in private and in the absence of the complainant. Nothing is said of the defendant's presence; presumably, Parliament did not intend to exclude him, and the application will be made to the court after members of the press and public have been excluded. Where such an application has been determined, the court must state in open court, but in the absence of the jury if there is one, its reasons for giving or refusing leave and, if leave is granted, the extent to which evidence may be adduced or questions asked. Presumably, this will also take place in the presence of the defendant, but in the absence of the complainant, who would otherwise be alerted to questions that she would face in cross-examination.

Cross-examination on previous inconsistent statements

A witness may be cross-examined about an earlier statement of his that is inconsistent with his testimony in court. In civil proceedings, a previous inconsistent statement will be evidence of the truth of its contents (s 6(1) of the Civil Evidence Act 1995). Similarly, in criminal proceedings s 119(1) of the Criminal Justice Act 2003 provides that if a person gives oral evidence and he admits making a previous inconsistent statement, or a previous inconsistent statement made by him is proved by virtue of s 3, 4 or 5 of the Criminal Procedure Act 1896 (c 18), the statement is admissible as evidence of any matter stated of which oral evidence by him would be admissible. (This is discussed further in Chapter 6.)

The manner in which a witness should be cross-examined about previous inconsistent statements is governed by provisions in the Criminal Procedure Act 1865, which applies to civil as well as to criminal proceedings.

Section 4 applies to both oral and written statements (*R v Derby Magistrates' Court ex p B* (1996)) and is declaratory of the common law. It provides that, if a witness who has made a previous inconsistent statement does not 'distinctly' admit that he has done so, proof may be given that he did make it. Before such proof can be given, the circumstances of the supposed statement, sufficient to designate the particular occasion, must be mentioned to the witness. The 'circumstances' include, for example, details of the time of the earlier statement, the place where it was made and particulars of other persons present when it was made (*Angus v Smith* (1829); *Carpenter v Wall* (1840)).

Section 5 applies to written statements only. Its effect is that a witness may be asked whether he made a statement and be cross-examined about its general nature without being shown the document. But, if the cross-examiner intends to use it as a contradictory statement, he must put it in evidence and the witness must be given the opportunity to explain the contradiction.

Re-examination

The object of re-examination is to clarify and complete any matters referred to in cross-examination and left in an ambiguous or incomplete state. It is not permitted to ask questions in re-examination unless they arise out of matters dealt with in cross-examination (*R v Fletcher* (1829)).

Refreshing memory

A witness may refresh his memory from a note while giving evidence if it is a 'contemporaneous' one. It need not have been made literally contemporaneously, but must have been made as soon as possible after the events, when they were still fresh in the witness' memory (*R v Richardson* (1971)). If the original note is not available, a transcript or later statement made from it may be used, provided it contains substantially what was in the note (*R v Cheng* (1976)).

'Refreshing memory' can refer to two different situations:

- where the witness' memory is actually jogged by the words on the page;

- where the events recorded were too long ago for the memory to be jogged, but the witness says that he is sure that the matters recorded are true (*Maugham v Hubbard* (1828)).

A witness may also refresh his memory outside court, before giving testimony, by re-reading his witness statement, even though that document was not made sufficiently contemporaneously to be used as a memory refreshing document in the witness box (*R v Richardson* (1969)). It is desirable, though not essential, for the prosecution to tell the defence if its witnesses have done this (*R v Westwell* (1976)). A witness who has begun to give evidence but has difficulty in remembering may try to cure this by interrupting his evidence and reading his witness statement silently, whether or not he read that statement outside court before going into the witness

box (*R v South Ribble Magistrates ex p Cochrane* (1996)).
However, he may not use the statement in the witness box
as if it were a contemporaneous note.

Where a contemporaneous note is used as a memory refreshing
document, the following rules, laid down in *Senat v Senat*
(1965), apply:

- cross-examining counsel may inspect the document. This
  alone will not make the document an exhibit;

- counsel may cross-examine on the document without making
  it an exhibit, provided the cross-examination does not go
  beyond the parts that were used to refresh the witness'
  memory;

- where cross-examination is on parts of the document not
  used to refresh the witness' memory, the document may be
  made an exhibit.

Where a memory refreshing document becomes an exhibit in
the case, the judge should direct the jury that it is not evidence
of the truth of its contents, but only of the witness' credibility
(*R v Virgo* (1978)).

Previous consistent statements

There is a rule, sometimes referred to as 'the rule against
narrative', that prohibits a witness from giving evidence that on
some occasion before trial he made a statement that is
consistent with his testimony at trial (*R v Roberts* (1942)).

Despite this rule, it is the practice to admit statements made by
an accused person to the police, even if they contain, either
wholly or in part, an exculpatory element.

A *wholly exculpatory statement*, though not evidence of the
truth of its contents, is admissible to show the attitude of the
defendant at the time he made it. This is not limited to
statements made on first encounter with the police, though the

longer the time that has elapsed since the first encounter, the less weighty the evidence is likely to be. It is the duty of the prosecution to present the case fairly, and it would be unfair to give evidence of admissions (which are admissible under s 76 of the Police and Criminal Evidence Act 1984), but exclude answers favourable to the defendant (*R v Pearce* (1979)).

A mixed statement (containing some inculpatory and some exculpatory parts) is also admissible. The judge should tell the jury to consider the whole statement when determining where the truth lies, but he should usually point out that excuses are unlikely to have the same weight as incriminating parts (*R v Sharp* (1988)).

Previous consistent statements are also admissible in the following circumstances:

- to rebut an allegation of recent invention (*R v Oyesiku* (1971); *R v Tyndale* (1999));

- where the statement was a 'recent complaint' in a sex case. To be admissible, the complaint must have been made as soon after the event alleged as could reasonably be expected; but this is liberally construed, and the personality of the complainant is taken into consideration in assessing reasonableness (*R v Valentine* (1996)). The mere fact that the statement was made in answer to a question does not make what was said inadmissible, provided the question was not of a leading nature (*R v Lillyman* (1986)). Since the sole value of the complaint is to show consistency, no evidence that it was made can be given if the complainant does not give evidence (*R v Wallwork* (1956)). In *White v R* (1999), the Privy Council held that a complainant may not give evidence of making a complaint unless the person to whom it was made is also called to prove its terms. In such cases, evidence of a complainant's distress shortly after or at the time of the complaint may also be given. This is similarly treated. It is admissible to show consistency with the description of the incident given in evidence by the complainant, but it cannot be regarded as confirming that evidence from an independent source (*R v Keast* (1998)). The judge in summing up should tell the jury that evidence of a complaint may possibly help them to decide whether the complainant is telling the truth, but that it cannot be independent confirmation of her evidence because it does not come from a source independent of her (*R v Islam* (1998));

● where the statement is part of the *res gestae* (see Chapter 7);

● as evidence of previous identification (see Chapter 8).

Hostile witnesses

A witness who fails to give the evidence expected of him may do so for honest reasons. Such a witness is merely 'unfavourable' and the advocate who calls him will have no remedy but to call other witnesses to give a different account of events. But, if the witness fails to say what is expected because he is not desirous of telling the truth to the court at the instance of the party calling him, he will be a 'hostile witness'. A witness ruled hostile by the judge may be cross-examined by the party calling him with a view to showing that he said something different on an earlier occasion (s 3 of the Criminal Procedure Act 1865; *R v Thompson* (1976)). However, he may not be cross-examined with a view to discrediting him by showing that he is of bad character (*Wright v Beckett* (1834)). A judge may conclude that a witness is hostile without a *voir dire*; it is within his discretion whether to hold one or not (*R v Honeyghon and Sayles* (1999)).

Collateral questions

A witness' answers to questions on 'collateral' (or ancillary) matters are said to be 'final', in the sense that evidence may not subsequently be adduced to rebut the answer given by the witness. However, note the following exceptions:

- by s 6 of the Criminal Procedure Act 1865, a witness' previous convictions may be proved where he denies them or refuses to answer;

- if a witness denies that he is biased, either for or against a party, evidence may be called to disprove him (*R v Phillips* (1936));

- evidence may be given of a witness' general reputation for untruthfulness (*R v Richardson* (1968));

- evidence may be given of a physical or mental disability affecting a witness' reliability (*Toohey v Metropolitan Police Commissioner* (1965)).

Protecting vulnerable or intimidated witnesses

Sections 16–33 of the YJCEA provide for special measures to protect vulnerable or intimidated witnesses. Witnesses may be eligible for assistance, either on the grounds of age or incapacity under s 16, or on grounds of fear or distress about testifying under s 17. A witness is eligible under s 16 if he is under the age of 17 at the time of the hearing, or the court considers that the quality of evidence given by the witness is likely to be diminished because the witness suffers from a mental disorder or otherwise has a significant impairment of intelligence and social functioning, or the witness has a physical disability or is suffering from a physical disorder. Under s 17, a witness other than the accused is eligible for assistance if the court is satisfied that the quality of evidence given by the witness is likely to be diminished by reason of fear or distress on the part of the witness in connection with testifying in the proceedings. A complainant in respect of a sexual offence is also eligible for assistance in relation to proceedings in respect of that offence.

The court may make 'special measures directions' in respect of eligible witnesses under s 19. It also has powers under s 21 to make special provisions for child witnesses, that is, witnesses under the age of 17 at the time of the hearing, if the trial is for one of the offences specified in s 35, which includes, *inter alia*, sexual offences and kidnapping. The primary rule in such a case is that evidence-in-chief must be video recorded and any evidence not given in that way must be given by means of a live link.

As well as video recorded evidence and evidence by live link, the special measures available to the court include screening the witness from the accused, excluding the public from court (but only where the proceedings relate to a sexual offence or it appears to the court that there are reasonable grounds to fear intimidation of the witness), removal of wigs and gowns and examination through an interpreter or some other intermediary. As a final sweeping up provision, s 30 provides that a special measures direction may provide for 'such device as the court considers appropriate with a view to enabling questions or answers to be communicated to or by the witness despite any disability or disorder or other impairment which the witness has or suffers from'.

By s 32, where on a trial on indictment evidence has been given in accordance with a special measures direction, the judge must give the jury such warning (if any) as he considers necessary to ensure that the accused is not prejudiced by that fact.

Sections 34–39 of the Act protect certain witnesses, such as complainants in trials for sexual offences and some child witnesses, from cross-examination by the accused in person.

Additional provisions under the Criminal Justice Act 2003

Section 51(1) and (2) provides that a witness (other than the defendant) may, if the court so directs, give evidence through a live link:

- during a summary trial;

- at an appeal to the Crown Court arising out of a trial;

- at a trial on indictment;

- at an appeal to the Criminal Division of the Court of Appeal;

- at the hearing of a reference under s 9 or 11 of the Criminal Appeal Act 1995 (c 35);

- at a hearing before a magistrates' court or Crown Court which is held after the defendant has entered a plea of guilty; or

- at a hearing before the Court of Appeal under s 80 of this Act (s 80 deals with retrials (see Chapter 18)).

Who can apply?

Section 51(3) provides that a direction may be given under this section on an application by a party to the proceedings, or of the court's own motion.

Will an application to give evidence via a live link always be successful?

Section 51(4) provides that a direction may not be given under this section, *unless*:

- a court is satisfied that it is in the interest of the efficient or effective administration of justice for the person concerned to give evidence in the proceedings through a live link;

- it has been notified by the Secretary of State that suitable facilities for receiving evidence through a live link are available in the area in which it appears to the court that the proceedings will take place; and

- that notification has not been withdrawn.

How does a court decide whether to allow evidence to be given via a live link?

Section 51(6) provides that the court must consider all the circumstances of the case. Section 51(7) provides that this includes such things as the availability of the witness, the need for the witness to attend in person, the importance of the witness' evidence to the proceedings, the views of the witness, the suitability of the facilities at the place where the witness would give evidence through a live link, or whether a direction might tend to inhibit any party to the proceedings from effectively testing the witness' evidence.

Refusal to make such a direction

Section 51(8) further provides that the court *must* state in open court its reasons for refusing an application for a direction under this section and, if it is a magistrates' court, must cause them to be entered in the Register of Proceedings.

Effect of and rescission of such a direction

Section 52 provides that once a direction has been given evidence can only be provided via live link. However, the court may rescind such a direction by an application by a party to the proceedings or of the court's own motion, if it appears to the court to be in the interests of justice to do so. However, an application may not be made unless there has been a material change of circumstances since the direction. Once rescinded, that person will no longer be able to give evidence through the live link unless another application to do so is made successfully. Section 52(7) provides that the court must state in open court its reasons for rescinding or refusing an application to rescind such a direction.

Magistrates' courts to sit at other locations

Section 53 provides that where it is agreed that evidence should be given by live link and a particular court is not suitably equipped, the court may sit for part or whole of the proceedings at an appointed place offering such facilities.

Warning to the jury

Section 54(1) provides that the judge may give the jury (if there is one) such direction as he thinks necessary to ensure that the jury gives the same weight to the evidence as if it had been given by the witness in the courtroom or other place where the proceedings are held.

4 Burden and standard of proof

Burden of proof

The 'burden of proof' is the obligation which rests on a party in relation to a particular issue of fact in a civil or criminal case and which must be 'discharged' or 'satisfied' if that party is to win on the issue in question. This burden is often referred to as the 'legal' or 'persuasive' burden, but must be distinguished from the *evidential burden* (see below).

Burden of proof in civil cases

In the absence of relevant case law or statutory provision, resort must be had, in doubtful cases, to general guidelines. Note especially the *dicta* of Viscount Maugham in *Constantine (Joseph) SS Line Ltd v Imperial Smelting* (1942):

- the burden should lie on the party who affirms a proposition, rather than on the party who denies it (but the courts avoid a mechanical approach to the 'affirmation or denial' test: see *Soward v Leggatt* (1836));

- the burden of proof in any particular case depends on the circumstances under which the claim arises.

In other words, where the burden of proof should rest is merely a question of policy and fairness based on experience in the different situations (*Rustad v Great Northern Rly Co* (1913)). In looking at those situations, a court will be concerned with, amongst other things, the ease with which a party may be able to discharge a burden of proof. See, for example, the following cases.

The Glendarroch (1894)

In a contract for the carriage of goods by sea, the shippers were exempt from liability for damage caused by perils of the sea, unless the damage was due to their own negligence. The goods were damaged when the ship became stranded.

Held: the owners of the goods had to prove the contract and non-delivery. The shippers had to show that the loss was caused by perils of the sea. It was then for the owners of the goods to establish the exception to that exception by proving that the shippers had been negligent.

Hurst v Evans (1917)

The plaintiff insured his goods against loss or damage by any cause, with the exception of loss or damage caused by the theft or dishonesty of his own servants.

Held: the burden of proof was on the plaintiff, when he made a claim, to show that his loss did not come within the exceptions.

Constantine (Joseph) SS Line Ltd v Imperial Smelting (1942)

Frustration was pleaded by shipowners as a defence to a claim by charterers.

Held: it was not necessary for the shipowners to prove that the frustrating event had occurred without fault on their part. The burden was on the charterers to prove negligence by the shipowners so as to bar them from relying on frustration.

Levison v Patent Steam Carpet Cleaning Co (1978)

The defendant cleaners relied on an exclusion clause when goods sent to them for cleaning were lost. This clause would not assist them if they had been guilty of a fundamental breach of contract.

Held: it was for the cleaners to prove that they had not been guilty of fundamental breach and not for the customer to prove that they had.

Pickford v ICI (1998)

The plaintiff sued her employers, ICI, in respect of cramp caused by her working conditions. She alleged that it was organic in origin and so foreseeable by ICI. ICI said that it was psychogenic in origin, and so not foreseeable. They called an expert who gave a particular reason for concluding that the

Burden and standard

Burden of proof

plaintiff's cramp was psychogenic in origin. The trial judge said that he was not satisfied that this expert's opinion was correct, but he also said that he was not satisfied that the cramp was organic in origin. He therefore found for the defendants. The plaintiff's appeal was allowed in the Court of Appeal, but that decision was reversed by the House of Lords.

Held: it had been for the plaintiff to prove that her cramp was foreseeable, not for the defendants to prove that it was not. She had failed to discharge her burden of proof and the trial judge's decision had been correct.

Burden of proof in criminal cases

The basic rule was laid down by Viscount Sankey in *Woolmington v DPP* (1935):

> Throughout the web of English criminal law one golden thread is always to be seen, that it is the duty of the prosecution to prove the prisoner's guilt.

Viscount Sankey said that the rule was subject to exceptions in the case of the defence of insanity, and subject also to any statutory exception. There is no problem in seeing where the burdens lie if a statute provides, for example, that an accused person shall be guilty of an offence 'unless the contrary is proved' (s 2 of the Prevention of Corruption Act 1916). However, the question whether Parliament in any given case has *impliedly* overruled *Woolmington* is more difficult to resolve.

By s 101 of the Magistrates' Courts Act 1980, where the defendant relies for his defence on any 'exception, exemption, proviso, excuse or qualification', whether or not it is part of the description of the offence, the burden of proving such a defence shall be on him. In *R v Edwards* (1975), the Court of Appeal held that this principle was not confined to cases heard in the magistrates' courts; the provision was a statutory statement of a common law rule applicable in all criminal courts.

In *R v Edwards*, Lawton LJ spoke of the need, when applying this principle, to construe the statute on which the charge was based to determine where the burden of proof lay. This task of interpretation was subsequently emphasised by the House of Lords in *R v Hunt* (1987), where it was held that the classification of defences for s 101 purposes was not constrained by the form of words used, or their position in the statute creating the offence. A more subtle approach to interpretation was required, which would pay regard to the wording of the Act, but would also take into account the mischief at which it was aimed, as well as practical matters affecting the burden of proof. Some guidelines were suggested by Lord Griffiths:

- courts should be very slow to classify a defence as falling within s 101, because Parliament can never lightly be taken to have intended to impose an onerous duty on a defendant to prove his innocence in a criminal case;

- the ease and difficulty likely to be encountered by the parties in discharging a legal burden are of great importance;

- the gravity of the offence must be considered.

But the task of interpretation is a difficult one, for at least four reasons:

- the question whether a given statutory provision falls within the class of 'any exception, exemption, proviso, excuse or qualification' is inherently problematic (see, for example, *Nimmo v Alexander Cowan and Sons Ltd* (1967));

- s 101 has been only haphazardly applied. Compare, for example, *Gatland v Metropolitan Police Commissioner* (1968) and *Nagy v Weston* (1965), and see offences under the Criminal Damage Act 1971;

- the project of distinguishing between rules and exceptions for s 101 purposes may be logically flawed because, rationally regarded, an exception is part of a rule;

- the reliance on policy that was authorised by *Nimmo v Alexander Cowan and Sons Ltd* (1967) and *R v Hunt* (1987) makes for uncertainty in interpretation.

The evidential burden

This is not strictly a burden of proof at all. It is best seen as a rule of common sense, which says that there must be *some* evidence for a particular issue to become a live one, so as to be fit for consideration by the jury or some other tribunal of fact. Whether an evidential burden has been satisfied is a matter solely for the judge.

In a criminal trial, the defence will have an evidential burden in relation to any issue that the prosecution are not required to raise. One obvious example is where the defence have a legal burden to satisfy in relation to any issue. But, although the defence do not, except for the defence of insanity, have a legal burden to establish common law defences, they may still have an evidential burden, for example, where the defence raised is that of self-defence (*R v Lobell* (1957)), duress (*R v Gill* (1963)), non-insane automatism (*Bratty v AG for Northern Ireland* (1963)) or provocation (*Mancini v DPP* (1942)). Note that the absence of consent in rape is an essential element of the offence, in respect of which the prosecution has both a legal and an evidential burden (*Selvey v DPP* (1970)).

Article 6 of the European Convention on Human Rights

It can be argued that imposing a legal burden of proof upon the accused may result in a violation of Art 6(2) (presumption of innocence). However, there appears to be no violation if imposing such a legal burden is reasonable and proportionate. In some circumstances, however, the court may be required to read the provision down under s 3(1) of the Human Rights Act 1998 as merely imposing an evidential burden.

Reasonable and proportionate

To determine whether a legal burden is reasonable and proportionate, it is necessary to consider whether the statutory requirement requires the accused to prove the relevant fact in issue, how difficult it will be for the accused to prove the relevant fact in issue, the potential offence with which he is charged, the accused's rights, whether requiring the accused to prove the relevant fact in issue achieves a fair balance between the public interest and the protection of human rights for the individual, and Parliament's view concerning what is in the public interest (*R v DPP ex p Kebilene* (1994)).

Imposing an evidential burden

This can be demonstrated in the case of *R v Lambert* (2001), which concerned a drug trafficking offence. Section 28(2) of the Misuse of Drugs Act 1971 raises the defence of 'knowledge', which essentially provides that if the accused was not aware he was carrying drugs then he could not have committed the offence. Where this defence is raised, it might be difficult for the prosecution to disprove it. However, the House of Lords felt that requiring the accused to prove the defence (that he did not have knowledge) was disproportionate, given the possibility of a life sentence should the accused be unable to prove this defence. Accordingly, in this case, the House of Lords held that the burden imposed upon the accused by the defence created by s 28(2) of the Misuse of Drugs Act 1971 was merely an evidential burden.

Standard of proof

The criminal standard

Two formulae are traditional. Jurors may be told, 'You must be satisfied so that you are sure', or 'You must be satisfied beyond reasonable doubt' of the defendant's guilt. However, it is the effect of the summing up as a whole that matters and the formulae do not have to be exactly followed, provided that their gist is explained to the jury (*R v Walters* (1969)).

Where there is a legal burden on the defendant to prove something in a criminal case, proof is required only to the civil standard (*R v Carr-Briant* (1943)).

The civil standard

A lower standard of proof is required in civil cases: proof on the balance of probabilities (*Miller v Minister of Pensions* (1947)). Where a serious allegation is made, for example, of conduct amounting to a criminal offence, proof is still only to the civil standard. The inherent improbability of such an allegation is taken into account when deciding whether the evidence is of sufficient weight to satisfy the court that the allegation has been proved. Earlier suggestions that a third standard existed, at some point between the ordinary civil standard and the criminal standard, were discredited in *Re H* (1996) by the House of Lords.

5 Presumptions

There are three types of presumption:

- presumptions of fact;
- irrebuttable presumptions of law;
- rebuttable presumptions of law.

Presumptions of fact

A 'presumption of fact' is no more than an inference from facts that is part of the ordinary reasoning process. For example, by s 8 of the Criminal Justice Act 1967, there is a presumption of fact that people intend the natural consequences of their acts. The section provides that a court or jury, in determining whether a person has committed an offence, shall not be *bound in law* to infer that he intended the result of his actions by reason of its being a natural and probable consequence of those actions, but shall decide whether he did intend that result *by drawing inferences from all the evidence*.

Irrebuttable presumptions of law

These are just the same as rules or principles of substantive law. For example, 'the presumption of innocence' is a way of referring to the principle that the burden of proof generally rests on the prosecution in a criminal case.

Rebuttable presumptions of law

The general pattern of these presumptions is that, once a party has proved certain basic facts, other facts will be presumed to exist, in the absence of some evidence to the contrary. The amount of contrary evidence required depends on the substantive law applying to the particular situation.

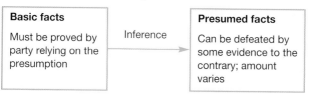

Basic facts		Presumed facts
Must be proved by party relying on the presumption	Inference →	Can be defeated by some evidence to the contrary; amount varies

Presumption of marriage

Where a man and a woman have gone through a ceremony of marriage followed by cohabitation, there is a presumption that the ceremony was valid. It was formerly held that the presumption could be rebutted only by evidence that went beyond a mere balance of probability (*Piers v Piers* (1849)), but the modern view of standards of proof suggests that rebuttal on the balance of probabilities would suffice (*Re H* (1996)).

Even where there is no evidence that a ceremony of marriage has been performed, a presumption that a man and woman were lawfully married will arise from evidence of cohabitation, coupled with their reputation as man and wife (*Re Taylor (Dec'd)* (1961)).

Presumption of legitimacy

There is a presumption that a child born or conceived during wedlock is the child of the woman's husband. The presumption applies not only where the husband and wife are living together, but also where they are living apart, whether by a formal or informal agreement. The presumption does not apply where the parties are separated by a court order but it will apply after the presentation of a petition for divorce or nullity, and even after the grant of a decree nisi (as opposed to a decree absolute) of divorce or nullity (*Knowles v Knowles* (1962)).

By s 26 of the Family Law Reform Act 1969, the presumption may be rebutted by evidence that shows that it is more

Presumptions

Rebuttable presumptions of law

probable than not that the person in question is legitimate or illegitimate, as the case may be.

Presumption of death

Some statutory provisions require a court to presume the death of a person in certain circumstances. There is also a common law presumption of death, as follows:

> Where as regards a certain person there is no acceptable evidence that he was alive at some time during a continuous period of seven years or more, then he will be presumed to have died at some time during that period if it can be proved that:
>
> - there are persons who would be likely to have heard of him during that period;
>
> - those persons have not heard of him; and
>
> - all due inquiries have been made appropriate to the circumstances.

(See *Chard v Chard* (1956).)

Res ipsa loquitur

This maxim, meaning 'the thing speaks for itself', was traditionally regarded as giving rise to some kind of presumption in actions for negligence. Where something which had caused an accident was shown to have been under the management of the defendant or his servants, and the accident was such as in the ordinary course of things did not happen if those who had management used proper care, the accident itself led to an inference of negligence (*Moore v R Fox and Sons* (1956)).

More recently, the maxim has been described as 'no more than an exotic, although convenient, phrase' to describe a common sense approach to the assessment of evidence. It means that a plaintiff *prima facie* establishes negligence where:

- it is not possible for him to prove precisely what was the relevant act or omission that set in motion the events leading to the accident; but

- on the evidence as it stands at the close of the plaintiff's case, it is more likely than not that the cause of the accident was some act or omission of the defendant, or of someone for whom the defendant is responsible, involving failure to take proper care for the plaintiff's safety.

It is misleading to talk of the burden of proof 'shifting' in a case where *res ipsa loquitur* applies. In any action for negligence, the burden of proof rests throughout on the plaintiff. In an appropriate case, the plaintiff will establish a *prima facie* case by relying on the fact of the accident. If the defendant adduces no evidence, there will be nothing to rebut the inference of negligence and the plaintiff's case will have been proved. However, if the defendant does adduce evidence, it must be evaluated to see if it is still reasonable to draw the inference of negligence from the mere fact of the accident (*Ng Chun Pui v Lee Chuen Tat* (1988)).

Presumption of regularity

This expression can refer to two different presumptions:

- the presumption that official appointments have been properly and formally made, and that official acts have been properly and formally performed, for example, *R v Verelst* (1813), where the defendant was charged with committing perjury while giving evidence in an ecclesiastical court, and it was held that the prosecution did not have to prove that the court official who administered the oath had been properly appointed. It was held in *Re v Dillon* (1982) that the presumption could not be relied on in a criminal trial to establish a central element of the offence charged. It is unclear whether the presumption, where it does apply, places a legal or merely an evidential burden on the person against whom it is to be used;

Presumptions

Rebuttable presumptions of law

- the presumption that a mechanical instrument, provided it is of a kind that is usually in working order, was in working order at a particular time that is relevant in the litigation. The effect of the presumption is to place an evidential burden only on the person against whom it is to be used. The presumption has been said to apply to watches and speedometers (*Nicholas v Penney* (1950)) and to traffic lights (*Tingle Jacobs and Co v Kennedy* (1964)). Evidence from computers, formerly regarded as suspect, is no longer subject to special provisions to ensure reliability, either in civil or criminal proceedings (see Sched 2 to the Civil Evidence Act 1995; s 60 of the Youth Justice and Criminal Evidence Act 1999). It seems to follow that the presumption of 'working order' now applies to computers, as well as to such instruments as watches, speedometers and traffic lights.

Presumption and the European Convention on Human Rights

Where a presumption operates against the accused in the context of criminal proceedings, this will not necessarily give rise to a violation of Art 6(2) (presumption of innocence). Whether there has been a breach of Art 6(2) will depend on whether the presumption lies within reasonable limits (*R v DPP ex p Kebilene* (1994)). In determining this, the court will consider:

- whether the presumption imposes a legal or evidential burden on the accused and whether it is a rebuttable or irrebuttable presumption;
- whether the presumption relates to an essential element of the offence;
- the purpose which the presumption serves;
- the nature and proof of the primary facts required to give rise to the operation of the presumption;
- the difficulty for the accused to rebut the presumption;
- what the accused has at stake and the rights of the accused (*R v DPP ex p Kebilene* (1994)).

6 Hearsay: evidence

Since the abolition of the hearsay rule in civil proceedings (Civil Evidence Act 1995), the rules restricting the admission of hearsay evidence are now only applicable to criminal proceedings. Part II, Chapter 2 of the Criminal Justice Act 2003 deals with hearsay evidence and will apply to all trials and other hearings such as Newton hearings beginning on or after 4th April 2005 (*R v H* (2005)). Hearsay is defined by s 212(2) of the Act 2003 as:

> a statement, not made in oral evidence, that is relied on as evidence of a matter stated in it.

Admissibility of hearsay evidence under s 114 of the Criminal Justice Act 2003

Section 114(1) provides that a *statement* not made in oral evidence in criminal proceedings is admissible as evidence of *any matter stated* provided that:

- any such admission is permitted by statute or common law;
- all parties to the proceedings agree; or
- the court is satisfied that it is in the interests of justice for it to be admissible. (See *R v Joyce and another* (2005).)

Note: the above is available to both defence and prosecution evidence.

Statement

Section 115 provides that a statement is any representation of fact or opinion made by a person by whatever means. It includes a representation made in a sketch, photo fit or other pictorial form.

Matters stated

Any matter stated is one to which the purpose, or one of the purposes, of the person making the statement appears to the court to have been to cause another to believe the matter, or to cause another person to act or a machine to operate on the basis that the matter is stated. On trial for conspiracy to kidnap, telephone entries were not a matter stated within s 115, but rather were implied assertions which were admissible because they were no longer hearsay (*R v Singh* (2006)).

In the interests of justice for it to be admissible

Section 114(2) provides that in deciding whether a statement not made in oral evidence should be admitted under this section, the court *must have regard* to the following (and to any others it considers relevant):

(a) how much probative value the statement has (assuming it to be true) in relation to a matter in issue in the proceedings, or how valuable it is for the understanding of other evidence in the case;

(b) what other evidence has been, or can be, given on the matter or evidence mentioned in paragraph (a);

(c) how important the matter or evidence mentioned in paragraph (a) is in the context of the case as a whole;

(d) the circumstances in which the statement was made;

(e) how reliable the maker of the statement appears to be;

(f) how reliable the evidence of the making of the statement appears to be;

(g) whether oral evidence of the matter stated can be given and, if not, why it cannot;

(h) the amount of difficulty involved in challenging the statement;

(i) the extent to which that difficulty would be likely to prejudice the party facing it.

Whilst the court *must* have regard to all of the above factors, there is no obligation to reach a conclusion on all nine factors. Instead, the court should give consideration to them and others which it considers relevant and assess their significance individually and in relation to each other (*R V Taylor* (2006)).

Principal categories of admissibility

Cases where a witness is unavailable

Under s 116(1) a statement is admissible as evidence of any matter stated, provided that that person's *oral* evidence would have been admissible, that the maker of such a statement (the relevant person) is identified to the court's satisfaction and that any of the five *conditions* as discussed below is satisfied.

Conditions – s 116(2)

The conditions are:

(a) that the relevant person is dead;

(b) that the relevant person is unfit to be a witness because of his bodily or mental condition;

(c) that the relevant person is outside the United Kingdom and it is not reasonably practicable to secure his attendance;

(d) that the relevant person cannot be found although such steps as is reasonably practicable to take to find him have been taken;

(e) that through *fear* the relevant person does not give (or does not continue to give) oral evidence in the proceedings, either at all or in connection with the subject matter of the statement, and the court gives *leave* for the statement to be given in evidence.

The relevant person is dead

Where one sole witness to an alleged crime died before trial, the admission of their statement made for the purposes of any prosecution that might ensue would not render the trial unfair (*R v Al-Khawaja* (2006)).

The relevant person is outside the United Kingdom

The term 'reasonably practicable' should be judged on the basis of the steps taken, or not taken by the party seeking to secure the attendance of the witness. However, this was only the first stage in determining admissibility. The court should also consider whether to exercise its exclusionary powers under 126 of the Act or s 78 PACE 1984. Whether it was fair to admit such statements would depend partly on what efforts should reasonably be made to secure the attendance of the witness, or at least, to arrange a procedure whereby the contents of the statements should be clarified and challenged (*R v C and another* (2006)).

Fear

For the purposes of sub-s (2)(e) 'fear' is widely construed and (for example) includes fear of the death or injury of another person or of financial loss. Where a court is sure that a witness for the prosecution does not give evidence through fear occasioned by the defendant, or persons acting on his behalf, then a statement made by such a witness may be admitted, even though the evidence may be the sole evidence against the defendant; but the court must be sure to examine the quality and reliability of the evidence (*Sellick v Sellick* (2005)).

Leave

May be given under sub-s (2)(e) only if the court considers that the statement ought to be admitted in the interests of justice, having regard to the statement's contents, to any risk that its admission or exclusion will result in unfairness to any party to the proceedings (and in particular to how difficult it will be to challenge the statement if the relevant person does not give oral evidence), in appropriate cases, to the fact that a direction under s 19 of the Youth Justice and Criminal Evidence Act 1999 (c 23) (special measures for the giving of evidence by fearful witnesses, etc) could be made in relation to the relevant person, and to any other relevant circumstances.

Business and other documents

Under s 117(1), a statement contained in a document is admissible as evidence of any matter, provided that such oral evidence would have been admissible, that the requirement of sub-s (2) is satisfied, and the requirements of sub-s (5) are satisfied, in a case where sub-s (4) requires them to be.

Sub-section (2)

(2) The requirements of this section are satisfied if:

(a) the document or part containing the statement was created or received by a person in the course of a trade, business, profession or other occupation, or as the holder of a paid or unpaid office;

(b) the person who supplied the information contained in the statement (the relevant person) had or may reasonably be supposed to have had personal knowledge of the matters dealt with; and

(c) each person (if any) through whom the information was supplied from the relevant person to the person mentioned in paragraph (a) received the information in the course of a trade, business, profession or other occupation, or as the holder of a paid or unpaid office.

Sub-section (4)

The additional requirements of sub-s (5) must be satisfied if the statement was prepared for the purposes of pending or contemplated criminal proceedings, or for a criminal investigation, but was not obtained pursuant to a request under s 7 of the Crime (International Co-operation) Act 2003 (c 32) or an order under para 6 of Sched 13 to the Criminal Justice Act 1988 (c 33) (which relates to overseas evidence).

Sub-section (5)

The requirements of this sub-section are satisfied if any of the five conditions mentioned in s 116(2) are satisfied, or the relevant person cannot reasonably be expected to have any recollection of the matters dealt with in the statement (having regard to the length of time since he supplied the information and all other circumstances).

Poor quality of evidence

Under s 117(7), the court may decide that a statement is not admissible if it is satisfied that the statement's reliability as evidence for the purpose for which it is tendered is doubtful in view of:

(a) its contents;

(b) the source of the information contained in it;

(c) the way in which or the circumstances in which the document concerned was created or received.

Common law categories of admissibility as preserved by s 118

See Chapter 7.

Inconsistent statements

Under s 119(1), if a person gives oral evidence and he admits making a previous inconsistent statement, or a previous inconsistent statement made by him is proved by virtue of s 3, 4 or 5 of the Criminal Procedure Act 1896 (c 18), the statement is admissible as evidence of any matter stated of which oral evidence by him would be admissible (*R v Joyce and another* (2005)).

Previous statements

Section 20 states that a previous statement by the witness is admissible as evidence of any matter stated of which oral evidence by him would be admissible, if:

(a) any of the three conditions below are satisfied; and

(b) while giving evidence the witness indicates that to the best of his belief he made the statement, and that to the best of his belief it states the truth.

Conditions

● The statement identifies or describes a person, object or place; or

● The statement was made by the witness when the matters stated were fresh in his memory but he does not remember them, and cannot reasonably be expected to remember them well enough to give oral evidence of them in the proceedings; or

● The following are satisfied:

- the witness claims to be a person against whom an offence has been committed;

- the offence is one to which the proceedings relate;

- the statement consists of a complaint made by the witness (whether to a person in authority or not) about conduct which would, if proved, constitute the offence or part of the offence;

- the complaint was made as soon as could reasonably be expected after the alleged conduct;

- the complaint was not made as a result of a threat or a promise; and

- before the statement is adduced the witness gives oral evidence in connection with its subject matter.

Types of statements admitted

These are statements made by the witness in a document, which are used by him to refresh his memory while giving evidence, on which he is cross-examined, and which as a consequence are received as evidence in the proceedings.

Similarly, statements rebutting a suggestion that a witness' oral evidence has been fabricated may be admitted.

Other considerations

Multiple hearsay

Section 121 provides that a hearsay statement is not admissible to prove the fact that an earlier hearsay statement has been made, that is, unless either of the statements is admissible under s 117 (business documents), s 119 (inconsistent statements) or s 120 (other previous statements), all the parties to the proceedings agree, *or* the court finds that it is in the interests of justice to admit the later statement.

Thus, unless a hearsay statement falls into either of these three categories, then one hearsay statement may not be relied on to prove, and may not be proved by, another hearsay statement.

Capability

Section 123 of the Criminal Justice Act 2003 concerns both the capability of the maker of a hearsay statement which is tendered under s 116, 119 or 120 of the 2003 Act and, in the context of a hearsay statement tendered under s 117, the capability of the person who supplied or received information or created or received a document. Section 123 provides that hearsay evidence will not be admitted if the person making or receiving a statement did not have the requisite capability to do so.

Credibility

Section 124 provides that evidence relevant to the credibility of the maker of the hearsay statement may be admitted in the same manner as if the maker of the statement had given direct oral evidence.

Expert evidence

Section 127 provides that a statement prepared for the purposes of criminal proceedings by a person who had personal knowledge of the matters stated may be used by another person (the expert) in evidence, provided notice has been given. The expert may thus base an opinion or inference on the statement and, if evidence based on the statement is given, then it is to be treated as evidence of what it states.

Unconvincing evidence

Where a case against a defendant is wholly or partly based upon a hearsay statement and such evidence proves to be so unconvincing that any conviction based on it would be unsafe, s 125 allows a court to stop a trial by jury at any time after the close of the case by the prosecution. In such circumstances, the court must direct the jury to acquit the defendant of the offence, order a retrial or discharge the jury.

General discretion to exclude

Section 126 provides that a court may refuse to admit hearsay evidence if the court is satisfied that the case for excluding it, taking account of the danger that to admit it would result in undue waste of time, substantially outweighs the case for admitting it, taking into account the value of the evidence. See *R v Joyce and another* (2005) where it was held that hearsay evidence consisting of previous inconsistent statements was appropriately admitted.

Section 78 discretion to exclude

In addition to the s 126 discretion, s 78 of the Police and Criminal Evidence Act 1984 (PACE) provides:

(1) In any proceedings the court may refuse to allow evidence on which the prosecution proposes to rely to be given if it appears to the court that, having regard to all the circumstances, including the circumstances in which the evidence was obtained, the admission of the evidence would have such an adverse effect on the fairness of the proceedings that the court ought not to admit it.

The Civil Evidence Act 1995

By s 1(1) of the Act, in civil proceedings, evidence shall not be
excluded on the ground that it is hearsay. Multiple hearsay, as
well as first hand hearsay, is admissible.

Sections 2–4 provide safeguards in relation to hearsay evidence.
There is a general duty on parties under s 2(1) to give warning
of the intention to adduce hearsay evidence. But by s 2(4)
failure to comply with this duty is not to affect the admissibility
of the evidence. Section 3 provides a power to call for cross-
examination a person whose statement has been tendered as
hearsay evidence. Statutory guidelines for weighing hearsay
evidence are provided in s 4.

Sections 5–7 are supplementary provisions. The maker of a
statement adduced as hearsay evidence must have been
competent to give direct oral evidence at the time that the
statement was made. There are provisions to admit evidence to
attack or support the credibility of the maker of a hearsay
statement, as well as evidence to show that the maker of the
statement made inconsistent statements, either before or after
the statement was made.

By s 8, where a statement contained in a document is
admissible as evidence in civil proceedings, it can be proved by
the production of the original document or a copy authenticated
in such a manner as the court shall approve. It is immaterial
how many levels of copying have taken place between the
original and the copy.

Section 9 concerns the proof of records of a business or
public authority. Its effect is that documents, including those
stored by a computer, forming part of such records are
admissible as hearsay evidence under s 1, and the ordinary
notice provisions apply. Unless the court otherwise directs, a
document shall be taken to form part of the records of a
business or public authority if there is produced to the court

a certificate to that effect signed by an officer of the business or authority. The absence of an entry in such records may be proved by affidavit of an officer of the business or authority in question.

7 Hearsay: common law exceptions

The following common law categories are preserved by s 118 of the Criminal Justice Act 2003 and so may be admissible in evidence.

1 Public information

This is admissible as evidence of the facts stated in them. For example, published works dealing with matters of a public nature (such as histories, scientific works, dictionaries and maps); public documents (such as registers, and returns made under public authority with respect to matters of public interest); records (such as the records of certain courts, treaties, Crown grants, pardons and commissions). Evidence relating to a person's age or date or place of birth may also be given by a person without personal knowledge of the matter.

2 Reputation as to character

Evidence of the accused's general reputation in the community is admissible for the purpose of proving his good or bad character. Evidence of good character is relevant to the accused's guilt, that is, because he is of good character he is unlikely to have committed the offence. Similarly, evidence of bad character appears relevant to the accused's guilt, that is, because he is of bad character he is more likely to have committed the offence.

3 Reputation or family tradition

Evidence of reputation or family tradition is admissible for the purpose of proving or disproving pedigree or the existence of a marriage, the existence of any public or general right, or the identity of any person or thing.

4 *Res gestae*

The Latin expression '*res gestae*' may be loosely translated as 'events occurring' or 'things happening'. If statement is said to be part of the *res gestae*, what is meant is that it is an out of court statement so closely associated with the circumstances in which it was made as to guarantee a greater reliability than usual. Such a statement is admissible as evidence of the matter stated if:

- the statement was made by a person so *emotionally overpowered* by an event that the possibility of concoction or distortion can be disregarded;

- the statement accompanied an act which can be properly evaluated as evidence only if considered in conjunction with the statement; or

- the statement relates to a *physical sensation* or *mental state* (such as intention or emotion).

Emotionally overpowered

These are spontaneous exclamations of the victim of an offence or of an observer. Although most of the cases are victims' utterances, this exception is not confined to them (*Milne v Leisler* (1862)). In *R v Andrews* (1987), the test for admissibility under this exception was laid down as follows:

- the primary question that the judge must ask is whether the possibility of concoction or distortion by the original speaker can be disregarded;

- to answer that question, the judge must first consider the circumstances in which the particular statement was made, in order to satisfy himself that the event was so unusual, startling or dramatic as to dominate the thoughts of the speaker to the extent that his utterance was an instinctive reaction to that event, giving no time for reasoned reflection. In such a situation, the judge would be entitled to conclude that the involvements or pressure of the event excluded the possibility of concoction or distortion, provided the statement was made in conditions of approximate contemporaneity;

- for the statement to be sufficiently spontaneous, it must be so closely associated with the startling event that the mind of the speaker was still dominated by that event. The fact that a statement was made in answer to a question is only something to be taken into consideration under this head; it does not mean that the statement will inevitably lack sufficient spontaneity;

- quite apart from the time factor, there may be special features in the case that relate to the possibility of concoction or distortion by the original speaker, for example, a motive of fabrication. Where a feature of this kind exists, the judge must be satisfied that there was no possibility of any concoction or distortion to the advantage of the speaker or the disadvantage of the defendant;

- the ordinary fallibility of human recollection may affect the weight of the testifying witness' evidence, but is not relevant to the question of *admissibility*. However, there may be special features giving rise to the possibility of error, for example, where the original speaker was drunk, or had made identification in particularly difficult circumstances. If there are special features such as these, the judge must consider whether he can still exclude the possibility of error before admitting evidence;

- where the trial judge has properly directed himself as to the correct approach to the evidence, and there is material that entitles him to reach his conclusions, the Court of Appeal will not interfere with his decision.

An *Andrews* checklist

- Was the nature of the event such as to make what was said an instinctive reaction to it?

- How close in time were the words of the event?

- Were there any special features to suggest that the original speaker might have given a *dishonest* account of the event?

- Were there any special features, apart from the fallibility of ordinary memory, to suggest that the original speaker might have given a mistaken account of the event?

Obviously, an 'excited utterance' argument cannot succeed where the utterance precedes that dramatic event by a significant period of time. See *R v Newport* (1998), where the utterance preceded the dramatic event by 20 minutes.

The nature of the event itself and the lapse of time between the event and the statement are likely to feature in arguments about admissibility. The less dramatic the event, and the greater the lapse of time, the less likely it will be that the speaker's mind was still dominated by the event, so as to rule out any opportunity for concoction or distortion.

Compare *Tobi v Nicholas* (1987) and *R v Carnall* (1995).

Physical sensation

The usefulness of this exception is limited, because while such statements are admissible as evidence of the sensations, they are inadmissible to prove their cause (*R v Gloster* (1888)).

Mental state

An obvious example is a defendant's expression of antipathy towards a murder victim shortly before the latter's death (see Lord Atkinson during argument in *R v Ball* (1911)). An expression of intention to do something has sometimes been relied on to prove that the speaker carried out the act in question (see *R v Buckley* (1873); *R v Moghal* (1977); but see also *R v Wainwright* (1875); *R v Thomson* (1912)).

5 Confessions

At common law, confessions are admissible to prove the matters stated.

6 Admissions by agents

Admissions made by an agent acting within the scope of his authority are admissible against his principal. An example of the agent/principal relationship would be a lawyer and his client, such admissions by agents are statements made by the agent to third parties: for example, statements made by counsel in open court and these are admissible as evidence of any matter stated.

7 Common enterprise

Where defendants are charged with conspiracy, or charged jointly with an offence where the prosecution alleges a common enterprise, evidence of acts done or statements made by one defendant in furtherance of the common enterprise will be admissible against those defendants, even though those other defendants were not present at the time when the act was done or the statement made. The reason for this is that a combination of persons for the purpose of committing a crime is regarded as implying an authority in each to act or speak in furtherance of the common purpose on behalf of the others (*R v Gray* (1995)). There must be independent evidence to prove that the defendant, against whom another's act or statement is to be used, was a member of the common enterprise (*R v Governor of Pentonville Prison ex p Osman* (1990)).

8 Expert evidence

Expert evidence is admissible provided the court requires it in order to make a decision in relation to a specific issue, which falls out of the court's experience or knowledge (*R v Turner* (1975)).

8 Hazardous evidence

Judges in the past attempted to control the way in which juries thought about kinds of evidence that were regarded as particularly unreliable. Early informal rules of practice later developed into formal rules of law about directions that should be given during a summing up. One of these sets of rules came to be known as the law relating to 'corroboration' which required juries to be warned about the danger of convicting on the 'uncorroborated' evidence of a witness in three types of case: where the witness was an accomplice, a child, or a complainant in a case where a sexual crime was alleged. The law of corroboration has now been very largely abolished by s 34(2) of the Criminal Justice Act 1988 (in relation to the evidence of children) and s 32 of the Criminal Justice and Public Order Act 1994 (in relation to evidence of accomplices and of complainants in sexual cases). The effect of these sections was stated by the Court of Appeal in *R v Makanjuola* (1995) to be that trial judges now have a wide discretion to adapt warnings about the testimony of any witness to the circumstances of the case. But for a warning to be given, there

must be some *evidential* basis for suggesting that the witness' testimony may be unreliable.

The *Makanjuola* approach can be applied where one defendant gives evidence that implicates another defendant (*R v Warwick Muncaster* (1999)). In practice, however, it seems that the Court of Appeal still expects a judge to give a warning where the evidence of a defendant implicates his co-defendant (*R v Jones* (2004)). Where a judge advises a jury to look for independent evidence that supports a particular witness' account, he should identify any independent supporting evidence (*R v B (MT)* (2000)). He should, presumably, also identify any evidence that is not capable of providing independent support if there is a danger that the jury might think that it does.

Despite the existence of this modern discretion, a body of case law has developed concerning warnings that a judge may be *bound* to give to the jury where lies have been told by a defendant. There also remains a body of case law about warnings concerning identification evidence, which has been unaffected by statute.

Evidence of a defendant's lies

Evidence of lies told by a defendant inside or outside court can have probative value, but will often require a direction from the judge to ensure that the jury approaches such evidence with care. The direction is sometimes still called a *Lucas* direction after a case in 1981 in which the problem was discussed in the context of the old corroboration law.

The law on the subject was stated more recently in *R v Burge* (1996). According to this decision, the direction should contain two points:

- the lie must be admitted by the defendant, or the jury must find it proved beyond reasonable doubt, before the jury can take it into account;

- the jury must be warned that the mere fact that the defendant has lied is not in itself evidence of guilt, because defendants may lie for innocent reasons. Only if the jury is sure that the defendant did not lie for an innocent reason can a lie support the prosecution case. The effect of this is that the prosecution has to negative any innocent explanation for the defendant's lie before the jury can take it into account in deciding whether the case is proved.

According to *R v Burge* (1996), a direction on these lines is usually required in four situations:

- where the defendant relies on an alibi;

- where the judge suggests that the jury look for something to support a possibly unreliable item of prosecution evidence, and points to an alleged lie by the defendant as potential support;

- where the prosecution tries to show that the defendant has told a lie, either in or out of court, about a matter apart from the offence charged, but which points to the guilt of the defendant on that charge;

- where the jury might adopt such an argument, even though the prosecution has not used it.

But a *Burge* direction is not required in every case where a defendant testifies merely because the jury might conclude that he told a lie about something while on oath. A direction will not be required where rejection by the jury of something the defendant said will leave them no choice but to convict. This will be the case where the prosecution evidence is in direct and irreconcilable conflict with the defendant's evidence on a matter central to the case (*R v Harron* (1996)), and may thus include in some cases, despite what was said in *R v Burge*, a lie about an alibi. In *R v Middleton* (2000), the Court of Appeal dismissed an appeal on the basis that to have given a *Lucas* direction would have confused the issue for the jury.

Identification and *Turnbull* guidelines

In *R v Turnbull* (1977), the Court of Appeal laid down guidelines for judges summing up in cases where the prosecution relies on contested identification evidence. Failure to follow the guidelines is likely to lead to the quashing of a conviction as unsafe.

When do the guidelines apply?

They apply whenever the prosecution case depends 'wholly or substantially' on the correctness of one or more identifications of the defendant, and the defence alleges that the identifying witnesses are mistaken. A *Turnbull* direction must be given in cases where identification is based on recognition as well as in other situations where there is a more obvious risk of error (*Shand v R* (1996)).

The need for a *Turnbull* direction generally arises where the issue is whether the defendant was present at a particular place or not. Where his presence at the scene is not disputed, but his participation in the offence is, the direction does not have to be given automatically. It will be necessary to give it where there is the possibility that the witness has mistaken one person for another, for example, because of similarities of clothing, colour or build (*R v Slater* (1995)), or because of confused action (*R v Thornton* (1995)).

Where the defence is that an identifying witness is lying, rather than honestly mistaken, the cases in which a *Turnbull* warning can be wholly omitted will still be exceptional. (But, for an example, see *R v Cape* (1996).) The judge should normally tell the jury to consider whether they are satisfied that the witness was not mistaken. But, in such a case, it will be enough to give the warning more briefly than in other cases (*Shand v R* (1996)).

A *Turnbull* direction almost certainly does not have to be given where evidence pointing to the accused is not evidence of *identification*, but only evidence of description, for example, where the witness observes only distinctive clothing or the general appearance of a suspect, such as his height and build (*R v Gayle* (1999)).

What does a *Turnbull* direction require?

A judge giving a *Turnbull* direction must do three things:

- warn the jury of the special need for caution before convicting the defendant on the evidence of identification;

- tell the jury the reason why such a warning is needed. Some reference should be made to the fact that a mistaken witness can be a convincing one, and that a number of such witnesses can all be mistaken. *R v Pattinson* (1996) suggests that there should be a reference to the risk of miscarriages of justice resulting from mistaken identifications;

- tell the jury to examine closely the circumstances in which each identification came to be made. But it is not necessary in every case for the judge to summarise for the jury all the weaknesses of the identification evidence. If he does choose to summarise that evidence, he should point to strengths as well as weaknesses (*R v Pattinson* (1996)).

Having warned the jury in accordance with the *Turnbull* direction, as developed in later cases, the judge should go on to direct the jury to consider whether the identification evidence is supported by any other evidence, identifying for them the evidence that is capable of providing such support.

It was said in *R v Turnbull* (1977) that, where the quality of the identification evidence is good, the jury can safely be left to assess it without any supporting evidence, subject to an adequate warning; but, where the quality is poor, the judge should withdraw the case from the jury at the end of the prosecution case unless there is other evidence to support the correctness of the identification.

Identifications inside and outside court

Dock identifications

It has been said that identification of a defendant for the first time when he is in the dock at trial is to be avoided (*R v Cartwright* (1914)). But, in *Barnes v Chief Constable of Durham* (1997), the Divisional Court acknowledged that such evidence was acceptable in magistrates' courts in certain cases.

Evidence of previous identifications

The evidence of a previous out of court identification of the defendant can be given by the person who made the identification, because it shows that the witness was able to identify the defendant at a time nearer to the events under investigation, so reducing the chance of mistake (*R v Christie* (1914)).

The rule against hearsay has been relaxed to allow evidence to be given by an observer of someone else's out of court identification, even where the witness who made the original identification has failed to remember in court that she identified anybody (*R v Osbourne and Virtue* (1973)).

Voice identifications

There is little authority on this subject. *R v Hersey* (1998) shows that a 'voice identification parade' can be held. In that case, the Court of Appeal said that, where there has been a voice identification, the judge when summing up must tell the jury of the risk of mistaken identification on lines similar to those adopted in cases of visual identification. However, in *R v Gummerson and Steadman* (1999), the Court of Appeal said that there is no *duty* to hold a voice identification parade since Code D of the Police and Criminal Evidence Act 1984 (PACE) applies only to visual identification. The court again said that voice identifications should be dealt with by suitably adapted *Turnbull* guidelines.

Code D of PACE

Breaches of this Code, which governs identification procedures, are likely to result in the exclusion of evidence because, if the Code is not followed, the reliability of the identification evidence is likely to be diminished. *R v Kelly* (1998) shows that failure to comply with the provisions of Code D will not lead inevitably to the exclusion of evidence.

There may sometimes be room for argument about whether Code D applies. In particular, the Code may not apply to identifications that are made only a short time after the commission of an offence (*R v Kelly* (1992); *R v Hickin* (1996)).

Even where the Code applies, failure to follow its provisions will not be fatal where to follow them would be futile. Thus, a suspect who requests an identification parade will normally be entitled to one, but, in *R v Montgomery* (1996) and *R v Nicholson* (2000), the Court of Appeal held that this was not the case where there was no reasonable possibility that a witness would be able to make an identification.

Code D contains provisions regulating the way in which identification by photographs should be made. But the fact that this means of identification has been adopted should not usually be brought out at trial by the prosecution because of what it will reveal about the defendant's background (*R v Lamb* (1980)).

Section 78 of PACE

Breaches of Code D may result in the exclusion of identification evidence in the exercise of the trial judge's discretion under s 78 of PACE. The judge should exclude such evidence if it is felt that its admission would have an adverse effect on the fairness of the proceedings (*R v Quinn* (1995)). Where a trial judge admits identification evidence in the context of such breaches, he should draw the breaches to the attention of the jury so that the jury can decide what, if any weight to give to the identification evidence (*R v Forbes* (2001); *R v Quinn* (1995); *R v Khan* (1997)).

'Forbes direction'

Following the House of Lords' decision in *Forbes* (2001), highlighting such breaches to the jury is referred to as a '*Forbes* direction'. The type of direction will vary depending upon the particular circumstances of the case and the nature of the specific breach of Code D. However, it will always be necessary to explain to the jury that there has been a breach of Code D, how the breach arose and to invite them to consider the possible effects of such a breach. Specifically, where a breach relates to a failure to hold an identification parade, the jury should normally be directed to the effect of holding such a parade. The jury should be told that holding an identification parade allows the accused to test the reliability of the identification witness' evidence and that in not holding such a parade the accused has thus been denied the benefit of the safeguard which an identity parade provides. The jury should be directed to take this factor into account and to give such weight to this as they think fair (*R v Forbes* (2001)).

9 Confessions and ill-gotten evidence

Although confessions are out of court statements adduced to prove the truth of their contents, they are admissible as an exception to the hearsay rule under s 76(1) of the Police and Criminal Evidence Act 1984 (PACE). However, it is recognised that considerations of fairness or reliability may make it undesirable to admit evidence of a particular confession or of some other item of prosecution evidence. Sections 76 and 78 of PACE deal respectively with confessions and with a discretion to exclude, for reasons of fairness, evidence on which the prosecution proposes to rely. To try to secure reliability and fairness, Codes of Practice have been created under ss 60(1)(a) and 66 of PACE. These attempt to control the ways in which certain types of evidence are obtained and breaches may lead to exclusion of an item of evidence under s 76 or s 78. The sections are often relied on in the alternative; in *R v Mason* (1988), it was held that s 78 applies to confessions as much as to any other kind of prosecution evidence.

By s 76(2), if in any proceedings:

- the prosecution proposes to give in evidence a confession made by an accused person; and

- it is represented to the court that the confession was or may have been obtained:

    (a) by oppression of the person who made it; or

    (b) in consequence of anything said or done which was likely, in the circumstances existing at the time, to render unreliable any confession which might be made by him in consequence thereof,

the court shall not allow the confession to be given in evidence *unless* the prosecution can prove that the confession (notwithstanding that it may be true) was *not* obtained in the circumstances referred to in (a) or (b) of the sub-section.

By sub-s (3), the court may of its own motion require the prosecution to satisfy it that a confession was not obtained in either of these circumstances.

By sub-s (4), the fact that a confession is wholly or partly excluded under sub-s (2) shall not affect the admissibility in evidence of any facts discovered as a result of the confession. By the same sub-section, where a confession has a relevance that goes beyond the truth of its contents, because it shows that the defendant speaks, writes or expresses himself in a particular way, so much of the confession as is necessary to show that he does so will be admissible.

Recognising a confession

By s 82(1) of PACE, 'confession' includes any statement wholly or partly adverse to the person who made it, whether made to a person in authority or not, and whether made in words or otherwise. An apparently wholly exculpatory statement does not amount to a confession if it becomes adverse to its maker because it appears to be evasive or because it is subsequently discovered to be false (*R v Sat-Bhambra* (1989)).

However, this decision was not followed by the Court of Appeal in the more recent case *R v Z* (2003). In this case it was said that whether or not a statement amounts to a confession will depend on whether or not it is adverse to the maker at the *time* it is tendered in evidence. This means that an initial statement which does not amount to a confession (because it is not adverse to the maker) may be subsequently tendered as a confession if by the time of the trial its contents have become adverse to the maker.

The partial definition in PACE assumes that a statement can be made by non-verbal means and there are cases that suggest that an admission can be made by conduct. In *Moriarty v London, Chatham and Dover Rly Co* (1870), a plaintiff's attempts to persuade several persons to give false evidence in support of his claim were held to be evidence of an admission by conduct that the case he was putting forward was untrue (see also *Parkes v R* (1976)). Even silence alone may amount to a confession if it can be construed as an adoption of an accusation by the person against whom it is made (see *Bessela v Stern* (1877), but see also *Wiedemann v Walpole* (1891)). Also, in *R v Batt* (1995), the failure of one defendant to dissociate himself from incriminating observations made by his companion was held to amount to evidence against him.

What one defendant says outside court when not in the presence of a co-accused will be evidence against the speaker, but not against the co-accused (*R v Gunewardene* (1951)), but such a statement will not automatically be 'edited' at trial so as to exclude the parts that are inadmissible against a co-accused. The judge has a discretionary power to exclude relevant evidence on which the *prosecution* proposes to rely so as to ensure a fair trial, but this does not extend to the exculpatory part of a mixed statement on which a *defendant* proposes to rely, for example, in which he has put the blame on another defendant (*R v Lobban* (1995)).

Note, however, that what one defendant says *when giving evidence in court* is evidence against a co-defendant whom it implicates (*R v Rudd* (1948)).

Excluding a confession under s 76 of PACE

Section 76(2)(a) provides for exclusion where the confession was, or may have been, obtained by oppression.

By s 76(8), oppression includes torture, inhuman or degrading treatment and the use or threat of violence (whether or not amounting to torture). This is an inclusive, rather than an exclusive, definition. Further guidance can be obtained from *R v Fulling* (1987), in which Lord Lane said that the word should be given its ordinary dictionary meaning, namely:

> Exercise of authority or power in a burdensome, harsh or wrongful manner; unjust or cruel treatment of subjects, inferiors, etc; the imposition of unreasonable or unjust burdens.

This quotation should not however be read as if it were itself a statutory definition; the context makes it clear that Lord Lane was emphasising the seriousness of the conduct envisaged. However, physical violence, or the threat of it, are not essential elements. In *R v Paris* (1993), it was held that interviews had been oppressive where a suspect had been verbally bullied.

The statute excludes a confession which was or may have been *obtained by* oppression. It therefore remains theoretically possible that there could be an instance of oppression that does not in fact cause a particular confession to be made. In those circumstances, the sub-section would not be available to the defence.

By s 76(2)(b), a confession will be excluded where it was, or may have been, obtained in consequence of anything said or done which was likely, in the circumstances existing at the time, to render unreliable any confession which might be made by the defendant in consequence thereof. The test is, therefore, one of *hypothetical* rather than *actual* reliability (see *R v Cox* (1991)).

With s 76(2)(b), as with s 76(2)(a), a causative link between the matters complained of and a confession must be shown, at least as a possibility, before there can be exclusion. The usual approach to s 76(2)(b) has been to say that 'anything said or done' had to refer to something said or done by some person other than the suspect (see, for example, *R v Goldenberg* (1989)). In *R v Walker* (1998), however, the Court of Appeal appears to have taken the view that the mere interviewing of a suspect is capable of being something 'said or done' for the purposes of this provision. Even if the line taken in *R v Walker* were not to be followed, there would still be room for a submission in favour of exclusion to be made under s 78 where the factors making for unreliability stemmed solely from the suspect who made the confession (*R v Anderson* (1993)). Even on the pre-*Walker* approach, once an external factor making for unreliability could be shown, it was then open to the court to take into account the personal circumstances of the person making the confession, because they are part of the 'circumstances existing at the time' which, by s 76(2)(b), are to be taken into account when considering reliability (see, for example, *R v McGovern* (1993)).

Where a defendant has made an admission that is vulnerable to s 76 at a first interview, a similar admission at a later interview may also be capable of being attacked, even though the original vitiating elements are no longer present, because the very fact of having made an earlier admission is likely to have an effect on the later interview (*R v McGovern* (1993)). However, the question is one of fact and degree and is likely to depend on whether the objections leading to the exclusion of the first interview were of a fundamental and continuing nature and, if so, whether the arrangements for the subsequent interview gave the defendant a sufficient opportunity to exercise an informed and independent choice as to whether he should repeat or retract what he said in the first interview or say nothing (*R v Neil* (1994); *R v Nelson and Rose* (1998)).

Confessions obtained after breach of a suspect's right to legal advice have very often been excluded. The right, which is set out in s 58 of PACE, is regarded as 'one of the most important and fundamental rights of a citizen' (*R v Samuel* (1988)). The case of *R v Alladice* (1988) was decided on its own exceptional facts which included an admission by the defendant on the *voir dire* that he was well able to cope with police interviews and had asked for a solicitor only to have a check on police conduct. It remains to be seen whether the availability of legal advice will retain its old importance now that inferences may be drawn from a suspect's exercise of his right to silence under the Criminal Justice and Public Order Act 1994 (CJPOA).

Section 76 at a glance

Section 76(2)(a)

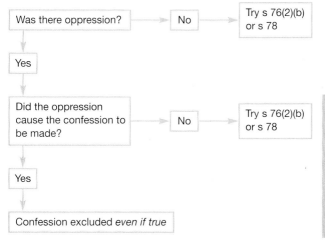

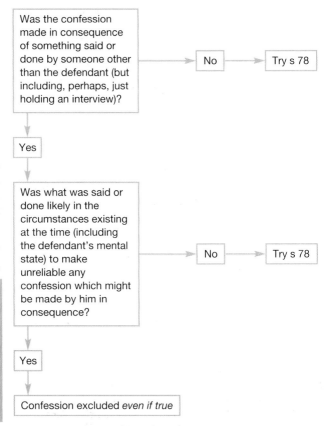

Section 78(1) of PACE

This sub-section provides that, in any proceedings, the court may refuse to allow evidence on which the prosecution proposes to rely to be given if it appears to the court that, having regard to all the circumstances, including the circumstances in which the evidence was obtained, the admission of the evidence would have such an adverse effect on the fairness of the proceedings that the court ought not to admit it.

The following points of interpretation should be noted:

- the evidence must be evidence on which the prosecution *proposes* to rely; it is too late to use the sub-section if the evidence has already been given (*R v Sat-Bhambra* (1989));

- it is not enough that the admission of the evidence will have *some* adverse effect; the adverse effect must be so great that the court ought not to admit the evidence (*R v Walsh* (1990)). However, once that stage has been reached, the judge must exclude the evidence – despite the use of 'may' in the opening words of the sub-section (*R v Chalkley* (1998));

- the 'fairness of the proceedings' refers only to that part of the proceedings taking place in court (*R v Mason* (1988));

- it is fairness of the proceedings that the judge has to consider. Fairness to the defendant is part of this idea, but so is fairness to the prosecution (*R v Robb* (1991)).

The exercise of the discretion

The Court of Appeal has given trial judges a very free hand in their operation of s 78(1) and has subjected their decisions to a minimum of review. In *R v Samuel* (1988), the Court of Appeal said that it was undesirable to attempt any general guidance as to the way in which a judge's discretion under s 78 should be exercised and in *R v Jelen* (1989) and *R v Roberts* (1997) the Court of Appeal made the same point, saying that this was not an apt field for hard case law and well founded distinctions between cases.

R v Chalkley (1998) suggests that the scope of a judge's powers under s 78 may be less wide than it appears to be from earlier cases and, in particular, may not extend to those cases where the evidence, though unlawfully or improperly obtained, is still reliable. It remains to be seen whether this will become generally accepted as the proper interpretation of s 78(1).

Several cases show that the Court of Appeal will interfere with a trial judge's exercise of his discretion under s 78(1) only for 'Wednesbury unreasonableness' (see, for example, *R v Christou* (1992); *R v McEvoy* (1997)).

In *Vel v Owen* (1987), the Divisional Court held that the prosecution does not have a burden under the sub-section to disprove unfairness in the way that it has a burden to disprove the existence of vitiating circumstances under s 76, but, in *R v Anderson* (1993), the Court of Appeal said that it was not entirely clear where the burden of proof lay on all the issues raised by the sub-section and, in *R v Stagg* (1994), prosecuting counsel accepted that it was for the prosecution to demonstrate either that there was no unfairness, or that its degree did not warrant the exclusion of the evidence.

A breach of one of the Codes of Practice may help to get evidence excluded under s 78(1). As the Court of Appeal said in *R v Elson* (1994), the Codes exist to protect the individual against the might of the State. The court added that the individual is at a great disadvantage when arrested by the police, and this is so whether or not the police have behaved with the utmost propriety. However, breach of the Codes will not lead to automatic exclusion of evidence (*R v Keenan* (1989); *R v Kelly* (1998)).

Even evidence obtained by a trick, or during an undercover operation, may be admissible (*R v Bailey* (1993); but see also *R v Mason* (1988)). In *R v Smurthwaite* (1994), the Court of

Appeal listed some of the factors to be regarded when considering the admissibility of evidence obtained during an undercover operation:

- Was the officer acting as an *agent provocateur* in the sense that he was enticing a defendant to commit an offence he would not otherwise have committed?

- What was the nature of the entrapment?

- Does the evidence consist of admissions to a completed offence, or does it consist of the actual commission of an offence?

- How active or passive was the officer's role in obtaining the evidence?

- Is there an unassailable record of what occurred, or is there strong supporting evidence?

- Did the officer abuse his undercover role to ask questions which ought properly to have been asked as a police officer and in accordance with the Codes?

Abuse of process

In relation to illegal, unfair or improper police conduct, the court may, where appropriate, stay the proceedings as an abuse of process (*R v Latif* (1996)). However, see also *R v Rotherham Magistrates' Court ex p Todd* (2000).

The common law discretion to exclude

The effect of s 82(3) of PACE is to retain the common law discretion to exclude evidence on the ground that its probative value is outweighed by its likely prejudicial effect. This is the discretion that operates in relation to the prosecution's right to cross-examine under s 1(3)(ii) of the Criminal Evidence Act 1898. Although potentially available in other circumstances, this is the only area where it is much used.

87

The common law discretion to exclude

Confessions

Use of confessions by a co-defendant

Section 76A of PACE (as amended by s 128(1) of the Criminal Justice Act 2003) provides that a confession may be given in evidence for a co-accused charged in the same proceedings, provided it is *relevant* to a matter in issue.

Unreliable confessions

Section 76A(2), however, provides that where it is represented to the court that such a confession was obtained by oppression, or as a result of something said or done so as to render the confession unreliable, then the court shall not allow the confession to be given in evidence for the co-accused, unless the parties can show on a balance of probabilities that this was not the case.

Section 76A(3) further provides that the court may of its own accord decide that before admitting such evidence it needs to be proven on a balance of probabilities that the confession was not obtained in this manner.

Facts discovered as a result of the confession

Section 76A(4) provides that if a confession is wholly or partly excluded, then this will not affect the admissibility of evidence of any facts discovered as a result of the confession, or where the confession is relevant as showing that the accused speaks, writes or expresses himself in a particular way, of so much of the confession as is necessary to show that he does so.

Failure to answer questions or mention facts

Under the CJPOA, there may be circumstances in which a suspect's silence, though not amounting to a confession, may be used as the basis for making inferences at trial.

Section 34 of the CJPOA

A court or jury may draw such inferences as appear proper from evidence that the defendant failed, on being questioned under caution, or on being charged with the offence, to mention any fact relied on in his defence if it was a fact which, in the circumstances existing at the time, he could reasonably have been expected to mention. The section applies to questioning by police officers, but also to questioning by other persons charged with the duty of investigating offences or charging offenders (s 34(4)).

When deciding whether a defendant could reasonably have been expected to mention a particular fact, consideration has to be taken of the *actual* defendant, with such qualities, knowledge, apprehensions and advice as he had at the time (*R v Argent* (1997)).

If a defendant says that he refused to answer questions on legal advice, that, by itself, is unlikely to be a sufficient reason for his failure to mention facts subsequently relied on in his defence. In practice, a defendant will have to go further and provide, either through his own testimony or that of his legal adviser, the reasons for the advice (*R v Condron* (1997)).

In *R v Gayle* (1999), the Court of Appeal held that s 34 does not apply to silence at an interview that took place in breach of any of the provisions of the Codes. By s 34(2A) of the CJPOA, where the accused was at an authorised place of detention, sub-ss (1) and (2) do not apply if he had not been allowed an opportunity to consult a solicitor prior to being questioned, charged or informed that he might be prosecuted.

The section requires that the defendant must have failed to mention some fact *that he relies on in his defence*. In *R v Moshaid* (1998), the defendant gave a 'no comment' interview and, at trial, gave no evidence and called no witnesses. The Court of Appeal held that s 34 did not apply because the defendant had not failed to mention 'any fact relied on in his defence at trial', but this was an unusual case. The House of Lords has recently said that 'fact' should be given a broad meaning (*R v Webber* (2004)). Thus, a belief formed by the accused upon the basis of information given to him by another may amount to a 'fact' (*R v Lydiate* (2004)). The accused may rely upon a fact by giving evidence of that fact himself or by adducing such evidence via examination-inchief or cross-examination of other witnesses. The accused may also rely upon a fact in his defence if it is put to the court in counsel's closing speech (*R v Webber* (2004)). Facts relied on may be established by prosecution witnesses in cross-examination or even during examination-in-chief, as well as by defence evidence (*R v Bowers and Others* (1998)). Note also where an accused gives a prepared statement to police but makes no comment in interview, this can amount to mentioning a fact (*R v Knight* (2003)).

The question of whether an accused has relied on a particular fact and, if so, whether he failed to mention it at interview is one of fact for the jury. There will, however, be cases where it is appropriate for a judge to decide, as a matter of law, whether there is any evidence on which a jury could conclude that either, or both, of these requirements has been satisfied. Where a judge has ruled that there is no such evidence, he should specifically direct the jury that they should not draw any adverse inference from the defendant's silence at interview (*R v McGarry* (1998)).

Where a defendant gives evidence that he refused to answer questions on legal advice, it may amount to a waiver of legal professional privilege. Whether or not the privilege is waived will depend upon the reasonableness of the accused's silence (*R v Condron* (1997)). It is thus irrelevant whether the advice was correct or incorrect, but rather whether it was reasonable for the accused to remain silent having regard to the nature of the advice and the context in which the advice was given. In this situation a lawyer/client privilege may well be waived and the prosecution may, during cross-examination of the accused or indeed his solicitor, explore the basis of, or the reasons for, the advice and the content of the lawyer/client conversation. Similarly, where an accused gives a 'no comment' interview upon the advice of his solicitor, this will not prevent the jury from drawing a s 34 inference if they believe that the accused's silence was because he had no, or no satisfactory explanation to give which was consistent with his innocence (*R v Hoare* (2004)). Similarly, where he goes further, for example, by eliciting evidence in cross-examination of a statement made to the police after the interview, setting out the grounds on which that advice was given, he will waive the privilege and can be cross-examined about the nature of the advice and the facts on which it was based (*R v Bowden* (1999)). The hearsay rule will be no bar to the admissibility of such evidence because it will be admitted to establish the effect of what was said on the defendant's state of mind when he decided not to answer police questions (*R v Daniel* (1998); *R v Davis* (1998)).

The scope for making inferences under s 34 was considered in *R v Daniel* (1998), which was followed in *R v Beckles and Montague* (1999). A jury is entitled to draw an adverse inference if they think the defendant's silence can only sensibly be attributed:

- to his unwillingness to be subjected to further questioning; or
- to the fact that he had not thought out all the facts; or
- to the fact that he did not have an innocent explanation to give.

Note: for the jury to draw an inference other than recent fabrication, they require an appropriate direction from the judge (*R v Petkar* (2003)).

Article 6 of the European Convention on Human Rights

In *Murray v UK* (1996), the European Court of Human Rights stated that a conviction should not be based solely or even mainly upon the accuser's silence. The court went on to say that the right to silence, though not an absolute right, remains a fundamental aspect of the fair trial procedure under Art 6 of the Convention.

Sections 36 and 37 of the CJPOA

These sections deal with inferences that may be drawn, in certain circumstances, from a defendant's failure to account for objects, substances, marks or his own presence in a particular place.

Inferences from refusal to provide samples

By s 62(10) of PACE, an adverse inference may be drawn from a suspect's refusal, without good cause, to consent to the taking of 'intimate samples' from his body. By s 65 of PACE (as amended by the CJPOA), an 'intimate sample' is:

- a sample of blood, semen or any other tissue fluid, urine or pubic hair;

- a dental impression;

- a swab taken from a person's body orifice other than the mouth.

'Non-intimate samples' may be taken, subject to procedural conditions, without a suspect's consent, and no provision corresponding to s 62(10) is therefore necessary.

10 Character evidence

For evidential purposes, the term 'character' can refer to a person's general reputation; their general disposition to behave in a particular way or to specific examples of misconduct, such as previous convictions. For legal purposes, a person is said to be of 'good character' if he has no previous convictions for criminal offences.

Good character

The common law rules governing the admission of evidence of good character are preserved by ss 99(2) and 118(1) of the Criminal Justice Act 2003 and provide that 'any rule of law under which in criminal proceedings evidence of reputation is admissible for the purpose of proving good character, but only so far as it allows the court to treat such evidence as proving the matter concerned'.

Evidence of good character in criminal proceedings

There are limitations on the sort of evidence that can be adduced for the purpose of showing that a defendant, because of his good character, is unlikely to be guilty. Under the rule in *R v Rowton* (1865), only evidence of general reputation is admissible as evidence of good character. (This includes the fact that the defendant has no previous convictions.) Evidence of the opinions of specific persons and evidence of specific good acts performed by the defendant are inadmissible. In practice, judges do not always keep strictly to these rules, but it is clear from *R v Redgrave* (1981) that any relaxation of the rule is an indulgence by the court and not a defendant's right.

The significance of good character

Where evidence of good character is given, its significance must be explained to the jury. Any judicial direction is now governed by rules laid down by the Court of Appeal in *R v Vye* (1993). This case recognised two 'limbs' about good character:

- the relevance of good character to credibility;

- the relevance of good character to the question of guilt or innocence ('propensity').

In addition, the court laid down the following rules to deal with various problem cases:

- when a defendant has not given evidence at trial, but relies in support of his defence on exculpatory statements made to police or others, the judge should tell the jury to have regard to the defendant's good character when considering the credibility of those statements;

- the second limb of the direction must always be given where the defendant is of good character. For these purposes, no distinction is drawn between defendants who have testified and those who have not. The judge should indicate that good character is relevant to propensity, but the actual words used are a matter for the judge in each case;

- a defendant of good character is entitled to a full direction, even if jointly tried with someone of bad character. In dealing with a co-defendant of bad character, a judge may *either* say nothing at all on the subject *or* tell the jury that they have heard nothing about the co-defendant's character and that they must not speculate about that or use it as evidence against him.

Failure to give a *Vye* direction where it is appropriate can lead to the quashing of a conviction (*R v Kamar* (1999)). In giving the direction, a judge is entitled to take into account the fact that, although without previous convictions, a defendant had previously been the subject of a formal police caution in respect of another offence. (This is not to be confused with the caution given to persons suspected of offences after arrest or before interview.) Since a pre-condition of administering this type of caution is an admission of guilt by the person cautioned, a judge may decide to direct the jury as to the relevance of the defendant's lack of previous convictions in relation to his credibility, but not to give the second limb of the direction in relation to propensity (R v Martin (1999)).

Doubtful cases of good character

Sometimes, a defendant will admit, as part of his defence, to *some* wrongdoing, though not that alleged by the prosecution. If he has no previous convictions, the *Vye* directions should usually still be given, subject to whatever qualification the judge thinks appropriate (R v Aziz (1996)). When a defendant has already pleaded guilty to some counts on an indictment, but is contesting others, the earlier pleas will generally mean that he is no longer of good character. Any direction about character in such a case will be a matter for the judge's discretion (R v Challenger (1994)).

Spent convictions and good character

With the leave of the judge, a defendant with spent convictions can be presented as a person of good character, provided the jury is not misled (R v Bailey (1989)). He can therefore be described as, for example, 'a man of good character with no relevant convictions'. Even if a conviction is not spent, it may be similarly overlooked if it is minor and of no significance in the context of the current charge (R v H (1994)). If an earlier conviction is ignored or, though mentioned, treated as irrelevant, the judge should give the *Vye* directions (R v H (1994)).

Bad character

Bad character evidence is dealt with in Part 11 of the Criminal Justice Act 2003 (CJA) which came into force on the 15 December 2004 and applies to all trials and Newton hearings which began on or after the 15 December 2004 (R v Bradley (2005)).

Definition of bad character – s 98 of the CJA 2003

This definition applies to both defendants and non-defendants and provides that any reference to "bad character" refers to evidence of, or of a disposition towards, misconduct on his part, other than evidence which has to do with the alleged facts of the offence with which the defendant is charged, or is evidence of misconduct in connection with the investigation or prosecution of that offence.

Section 112(1) of the CJA 2003

Section 112(1) defines 'misconduct' as 'the commission of an offence or other reprehensible behaviour' (*R v Manister* (2005) and *R v Hong Quang* (2005)). The definition is broad and will incorporate: evidence of previous convictions; evidence of other charges being tried concurrently; evidence of previous charges not pursued by the prosecution and acquittals.

More than one offence on the indictment

Section 112(2) provides that where a defendant is charged with two or more offences in the same proceedings, each offence on the indictment is treated as if it was charged in separate proceedings. The effect of this is that if the prosecution wish to adduce evidence of the alleged facts of one offence with which the defendant is charged then this will be treated as bad character evidence for the purposes of admissibility in relation to one or more of the other offences with which he is charged on the indictment.

Persons other than the defendant: non-defendant's bad character

The bad character evidence of the non-defendant is governed by s 100 of the CJA 2003. Non-defendants are not actually defined in the Act but include victims, whether or not they give evidence, witnesses and third parties who are not witnesses in the case. The provisions make no distinction between defendants who are witnesses and others who are strangers to the proceedings.

Leave of the court

Unless evidence is being adduced under s 101(1)(c) (all the parties to the proceedings agree to the evidence being admissible), evidence of the bad character of a person other than the defendant must not be given without leave of the court. In deciding whether to grant leave, the court must have regard to section s 100(1).

Section 100(1) provides that for bad character of a person other than the defendant to be admissible it must either be:

(a) important explanatory evidence, or

(b) of substantial *probative value* in relation to a matter which:

   (i) is a matter in issue in the proceedings, and

   (ii) is of substantial importance in the context of the case as a whole.

Important explanatory evidence

This is essentially background evidence and s 100(2) provides that without such evidence, the court or jury would find it impossible or difficult to properly understand the other evidence in the case, and its value for understanding the case as a whole is substantial (*R v Akram* (2005)).

Substantial probative value

Section 100(3) provides that when the court is assessing the probative value of evidence, it must have regard to the nature and number of the events, or other things, to which the evidence relates and to when those events or things are alleged to have happened or existed (*Razaq and Razaq* (2005)). Where evidence is evidence of misconduct the court must consider the nature and extent of the similarities and the dissimilarities between each of the alleged instances of misconduct and the extent to which the evidence shows or tends to show that the same person was responsible each time. The court may also consider other factors which it feels are relevant.

Credibility of a witness

The credibility of a prosecution witness may have substantial probative value in relation to a matter in the proceedings and is of substantial importance in the context of the case as a whole (*Yaxlev-Lennon* (2005) and *Osbourne* (2005)).

A defendant's bad character

Leave to adduce evidence of a defendant's bad character is not required. This is in contrast to the non-defendant (previously discussed) where, unless all parties agreed, leave to adduce such evidence is required by the court. Instead, if the prosecution intend to adduce evidence of a defendant's (or co-defendant's bad character) they should serve notice to the defence (s 111(2)) indicating the nature of the bad character evidence and the prescribed 'gateway' under s 101(1)) through which they intend to adduce the evidence.

The seven gateways

Under s 101(1) evidence of the defendant's bad character in criminal proceedings is *only* admissible if:

1 All the parties to the proceedings agree to the evidence being admissible (s 101(1)(a))

This section accommodates for the situation where all parties agree that the evidence should be admitted.

2 The evidence is adduced by the defendant himself or is given in answer to a question asked by him in cross-examination and intended to elicit it (s 101(1)(b))

A defendant may choose to admit such evidence himself during examination in an attempt to persuade a jury to look upon him more favourably and possibly as someone with nothing to hide. Similarly a defendant might feel that adducing his bad character might be helpful to his case, for example, where a defendant raises an alibi and that alibi involves evidence of bad character in some way.

3 It is important explanatory evidence (s 101(1)(c))

Section 102 defines 'important explanatory evidence' as evidence, without which, the court or jury would find it impossible or difficult properly to understand, other evidence in the case, and its value for understanding the case as a whole is substantial. This is the same definition as important explanatory evidence in s 100(2) when dealing with non-defendant's bad character. If the evidence is more than minor or more than trivial it will be admissible if it assists the court to understand the case as a whole.

4 It is relevant to an important matter in issue between the defendant and his prosecution (s 101(1)(d))

Section 103(1) provides matters in issue between the defendant and the prosecution include the question whether the defendant has a propensity to commit offences of the kind with which he is charged, except where his having such a propensity makes it no more likely that he is guilty of the offence. Similarly it includes the question whether the defendant has a propensity to be untruthful, except where it is not suggested that the defendant's case is untruthful in any respect.

Definition of propensity

Section 103(2) suggests that, apart from any other means, a defendant's propensity to commit offences of the kind with which he is charged may be established by evidence that he has been convicted of:

(a) an offence of the same description as the one with which he is charged, or

100

(b) an offence of the same category as the one with which he is charged.

Currently to date only two such 'categories of offences' have been prescribed, namely the 'theft category' (Criminal Justice Act 2003 (Categories of Offences) Order 2004 (SI 2004/3346)); and the 'sexual offences category.' (persons under the age of 16) (Criminal Justice Act 2003 (Categories of Offences) Order 2004 (SI 2004/3346)).

Propensity to commit offences

Section 103(2) makes clear that this does not prevent the admission of convictions which are neither of the same description nor the same category from being relied upon as evidence of a defendant's propensity to commit offences of the kind which he is charged. The test is not simply whether the defendant has committed the offence(s) in question but rather whether he has a (presumably current) propensity to commit such offences (*Hanson, Gilmore, Pickstone* (2005)).

Propensity to be untruthful

Propensity to be untruthful relates to the way in which the defendant has or is currently conducting his defence. This will apply, for example, where a defendant has previously been tried for an offence having pleaded not guilty and then convicted of the offence. This evidence will be potentially admissible to demonstrate a propensity to be untruthful and that he cannot be regarded as a credible witness. Under s 103(1)(b), propensity becomes admissible to prove untruthfulness, provided that the prosecution contends that the defendant's case is untruthful in some respect (*R v Somanathan*) and such evidence would not therefore be admissible to prove a propensity to be untruthful where it is not alleged that the defendant's case is untruthful in any respect (s 103(1)(b)).

A defendant's bad character

Character evidence

Excluded evidence

Section 101(3) provides that the court must not admit evidence that is relevant to an important matter in issue between the defendant and his prosecution if, on application by the defendant to exclude it, it appears to the court that the admission of the evidence would have such an adverse effect on the fairness of the proceedings that the court ought not to admit it. Once relevance has been established, the judge should then perform a balancing exercise in order to determine whether the evidence have such an adverse effect on the fairness of the proceedings that the court ought not to admit it (*R v Somanathan* (2005)).

5 It has substantial probative value in relation to an important matter in issue between the defendant and a co-defendant (s 101(1)(e))

Only a co-defendant and not the prosecution can adduce evidence of a defendant's bad character under this section. Once a defendant has given evidence against a co-accused, any subsequent cross-examination of the defendant will be restricted to that which is 'relevant to a matter in issue' and is subject to the 'enhanced relevance test'.

Propensity to be untruthful

Where evidence relates to a co-defendant's propensity to be untruthful, s 104(1) provides that evidence which is relevant to the question whether the defendant has a propensity to be untruthful is admissible only if the nature or conduct of his defence is such as to undermine the co-defendant's defence and where the question of that co-defendant's truthfulness is truly relevant to the case for the defendant.

6 It is evidence to correct a false impression given by the defendant (s 101(1)(f))

Section 105(1)(a) provides that a defendant gives a false impression if he is responsible for making an express or implied assertion which is apt to give the court a false or misleading impression about himself. Section 105(2) further provides that a defendant is treated as being responsible for the making of an assertion if:

(a) the assertion is made by the defendant in the proceedings (whether or not in evidence given by him);

(b) the assertion was made by the defendant:

   (i) on being questioned under caution, before charge, about the offence with which he is charged, or

   (ii) on being charged with the offence or officially informed that he might be prosecuted for it, and the evidence of the assertion is given in the proceedings;

(c) the assertion is made by a witness called by the defendant;

(d) the assertion is made by the defendant that is intended to elicit it, or is likely to do so; or

(e) the assertion was made by a person out of court, and the defendant adduces evidence of it in the proceedings.

Disassociation

Section 105(3) provides that a defendant who would otherwise be treated as responsible for the making of an assertion shall not be so treated if he withdraws it or disassociates himself from it. However, a confession extracted in cross-examination where a defendant was not telling the truth in his examination in chief would not normally amount to a withdrawal or disassociation (*R v Renda* (2005)).

7 The defendant has made an attack on another person's character (s 101(1)(d))

Section 106(1) provides that a defendant makes an attack on another person's character if:

(a) he adduces evidence attacking the other persons character;

A defendant's bad character

Character evidence

(b) he (or any legal representative appointed under s 38 (4) of the Youth Justice and Criminal Evidence Act 1999 (c 23)) asks questions in cross-examination that are intended to elicit such evidence, or are likely to do so; or

(c) evidence is given of an imputation about the other person made by the defendant on being questioned under caution, before charge, about the offence with which he is charged, or on being charged with the offence or officially informed that he might be prosecuted for it.

Section 106(2) provides that evidence which attacks another person's character means evidence to the effect that the other person has committed an offence, whether a different offence from the one with which the defendant is charged or the same one, or has behaved, or is disposed to behave, in a reprehensible way (*R v Ball* (2005)).

Excluded evidence

Section 101(3) provides that the court must not admit evidence where the defendant has made an attack on another person's character if, on application by the defendant to exclude it, it appears to the court that the admission of the evidence would have such an adverse effect on the fairness of the proceedings that the court ought not to admit it. There is no requirement in the Act that the attack on the other person's character should be untrue or unfounded. However, where it can be shown that those allegations are true, then the court may exercise its discretion and exclude the evidence of bad character on the basis that it is fair to do so.

Once evidence has been admitted through a particular gateway, to what purpose can evidence then be used?

Once evidence of bad character has been admitted through one of the 'gateways' in the Criminal Justice Act 2003 (s 101(1)), the use to which it could be put depends upon the matters to which it was relevant rather than the upon the gateway through which it was admitted (*R v Edward Paul Highton; R v Dong Van Nguyen; and R v Anthony Carp* (2005)).

Discretion to exclude under s 78 of PACE

Section 101(3) is applicable to only evidence adduced under sub-ss 101(d) and (g) and is designed to reflect the existing position under s 78 of PACE, under which the judge or magistrates assess the probative value of the evidence to an issue in the case and the prejudicial effect of admitting it, and excludes the evidence where it would be unfair to admit it. However, the test to be applied under s 101(3) is stricter than that under s 78 of PACE in that under s 78 the court *may* refuse to admit the evidence, whereas under s 101(3) the *court must not* admit such evidence if it would have such an adverse effect on the fairness of the proceedings. Other than in s 101(e), which is subject to the 'enhanced relevance' test in any event, it is submitted that s 78 of PACE will continue to apply to the other gateways.

Stopping the case where evidence is contaminated

Section 107(5)(b) provides that evidence is contaminated where it is false or misleading in any respect, or is different from what it would otherwise have been. Section 107(1) provides that if during a defendant's trial before a judge and jury for an offence, evidence of his bad character has been admitted under any of the paragraphs (c) to (g) of s 101(1), and the court is satisfied at any time after the close of the case for the prosecution that the evidence is contaminated and the contamination is such that, considering the importance of the evidence to the case against the defendant, his conviction of the offence would be unsafe, the court must direct the jury to acquit the defendant of the offence, or if it considers that there ought to be a retrial, discharge the jury offence.

Effect of s 107

This provision does not affect any existing court powers in relation to ordering an acquittal or discharging a jury. Instead the effect of s 107 is to further supplement those powers by conferring a duty on the judge to stop the case if the contamination is such that, considering the importance of the evidence to the case, a conviction would be unsafe.

Offences committed by a defendant when a child

Section 108(2) provides that in proceedings for an offence committed or alleged to have been committed by the defendant when aged 21 or over, evidence of his conviction for an offence when under the age of 14 is not admissible unless:

(a) both of the offences are triable only on indictment, and

(b) the court is satisfied that the interests of justice require the evidence to be admissible.

These factors are *additional* to those factors outlined in s 101 (defendant's bad character) as discussed above.

Other considerations

Notice

The prosecution must give notice to the defence if it seeks to rely on bad character evidence. This is irrespective of how it is presented to the court and the notice requirement will equally apply if the prosecution seek to adduce such information by way of cross-examination (s 111(2)). If notice is not given, then the court may exercise its powers with respect to costs (s 111(4)).

Relevant ruling

Relevant ruling means a ruling on whether an item of evidence is evidence of a person's bad character and whether such evidence is admissible under s 100 (non-defendant's bad character) or s 101 (defendant's bad character). The court may also make a ruling under s 101(3) and decide that it would be unfair to admit evidence or under s 107 where the court decides to stop the case where evidence is contaminated.

Court's duty to give reasons for rulings

Section 110 provides that where a court makes a relevant ruling, it must state in open court (but in the absence of the jury, if there is one), its reasons for the ruling. If it is a Magistrates' Court, it must cause the ruling and the reasons for it to be entered in the register of the court's proceedings.

Assumption of truth

Section 109 provides that any reference to relevance or probative value of evidence is on the assumption that such evidence is true. In assessing the relevance or probative value of an item of evidence, a court may not assume that the evidence is true if it appears, on the basis of any material before the court (including any evidence it decides to hear on the matter), that no court or jury could reasonably find it to be true.

Other considerations

107

Character evidence

11 Opinion evidence

The main topics of importance are: (a) the circumstances in which opinion evidence is generally admissible; (b) analysing the basis on which an opinion has been given; and (c) the extent to which the evidence of psychiatrists or psychologists is admissible in criminal trials.

When is opinion evidence admissible?

The fundamental rule is that witnesses testify about facts and not about the opinions they have formed from facts. The reason for this is the idea that it is the job of the 'tribunal of fact' (a judge or, very occasionally, a jury in a civil case, and magistrates or a jury in a criminal case) to hear the evidence, find facts, and make inferences from them. For this reason a witness should not generally be asked to give his opinion about what another witness has said (*R v Windass* (1989)).

By s 3(2) of the Civil Evidence Act 1972, a person called as a witness in civil proceedings may give a statement of opinion on any matter on which he is not qualified to give expert evidence, if that statement is made as a way of conveying relevant facts personally perceived by him.

The main exception to the fundamental rule is that in both civil and criminal cases an expert may give evidence of his opinion where the matters on which he testifies are likely to be outside the experience of judge or jury. In *R v Stockwell* (1993), the Court of Appeal said that in each case it is for the judge to decide:

- whether the issue is one on which the court could be assisted by expert evidence;

- whether the expert tendered has the expertise to provide such evidence.

While a witness giving such evidence should be skilled in the subject, there are no restrictions on the manner in which that skill has to be acquired. The evidence of a person without professional qualifications can be admitted, provided that the judge is satisfied that the witness is sufficiently skilled (*R v Silverlock* (1894)). So, a witness who has acquired his expertise in the course of his daily work may give expert evidence even though he lacks paper qualifications. See, for example, *R v Murphy* (1980), where a police constable who was a traffic accident expert was allowed to give evidence of his opinion as to the nature of a collision, the course of one of the vehicles involved and other matters said to be deducible from marks in the road and damage to the vehicles.

A witness who is otherwise not specially qualified may be an 'expert *ad hoc*' where he has special knowledge acquired by study of materials that are relevant in a particular case, such as video recordings or photographs (*R v Clare and Peach* (1995)).

Although it is clear that the object of expert evidence is to provide the court with information that is outside the experience of judge or jury, there is little authority on how to determine whether particular information falls within this class. A case where a problem did arise (though it was not the central problem) was *R v Stagg* (1994), where the trial judge doubted whether evidence obtained from the technique known as 'psychological profiling' was expert evidence of a kind recognised by the courts.

The basis of the opinion

An expert gives his opinion on the basis of facts in a particular case but those facts must themselves be proved by admissible evidence. However, if the rule against hearsay was strictly applied, an expert would often be prevented from giving an opinion because his reasoning and conclusions would be governed by matters that he had learned in the course of his training and experience, either from what he had read, or from others who share his specialisation. The courts have therefore relaxed the hearsay rule to take this into account (*Abbey National Mortgages plc v Key Surveyors Nationwide Ltd* (1996)).

Experts may support their opinions by referring to articles, letters, journals and other materials, whether published or not, when giving their testimony. Where they have done so, however, this should be mentioned in their evidence so that it can be taken into account when considering the probative worth of their opinion as a whole (*R v Abadom* (1983)).

Sometimes the primary facts of a case are not established by the expert himself, but by other members of a team, which the expert leads. In such a case, the evidence of the other relevant team members must be available (in the absence of formal admissions), so that the primary facts can all be proved by admissible evidence (*R v Jackson* (1996)).

By s 30(1) of the Criminal Justice Act 1988, an 'expert report' (that is, a written report by a person dealing wholly or mainly with matters on which he is, or, if living, would be, qualified to give expert evidence) shall be admissible as evidence in criminal proceedings, whether or not the person making it attends to give oral evidence. If it is proposed that the person making the report shall not give oral evidence, the report shall be admissible only with leave of the court (but it seems most unlikely that a court would allow an expert report to be adduced without calling the maker if the opposing party had a genuine desire to cross-examine on it).

Evidence from psychiatrists and psychologists

To some extent judges recognise that a psychiatrist or psychologist may be able to provide useful testimony about matters that are outside the experience of judge or jurors (see, for example, *DPP v A and BC Chewing Gum Ltd* (1968), which concerned the effect of certain articles on children, and *R v Morris* (1998), in which the Court of Appeal held that expert evidence is required where it is alleged that psychiatric illness or injury resulted from a defendant's non-physical assault).

There is also a fear that mental experts will usurp the role of the jury or other triers of fact unless a clear line is drawn between abnormal and normal mental states. One effect of this has been to draw a distinction between expert evidence relevant to the reliability of a confession and expert evidence relevant to *mens rea*. Judges regularly admit psychiatric or psychological evidence when considering submissions about the admissibility of confessions, because the mental condition of the defendant at the time of interview is one of the circumstances to be considered under s 76(2)(b) of the Police and Criminal Evidence Act 1984 (*R v Raghip* (1991)). In *R v Walker* (1998), it was held that nothing limits the form of mental or psychological condition on which a defendant can rely to show that his confession is unreliable. However, in *R v O'Brian and Others* (2000), the Court of Appeal said that, while it had been accepted that expert evidence was admissible if it demonstrated some abnormality relevant to the reliability of a defendant's confession:

- the abnormal disorder must not only be of the type which might render a confession unreliable, but there must also be a very significant deviation from the norm; and

- there should be a history pre-dating the making of admissions which was not based solely on an account given by the defendant and which pointed to or explained the abnormality.

In *R v Coles* (1995), the Court of Appeal held that expert evidence is inadmissible to enable a jury to reach a decision about the existence of *mens rea, unless related to the mental health or psychiatric state of the defendant*. Thus, jurors have been held to be sufficiently acquainted with how ordinary people are likely to react to the stresses and strains of life (*R v Turner* (1975); but see also *R v Lowery* (1974)). Similarly, they are not allowed to have expert evidence to tell them whether a person, not suffering from some defect or abnormality of mind, is likely to be telling the truth (*R v Mackenney* (1981)).

Where psychiatric evidence does not suggest any organic or psychiatric connection between the defendant's medical condition and his inability at the material time to commit the crime, the evidence will be inadmissible, since it will go to prove the probability of the defendant's truthfulness, as opposed to providing relevant information likely to be outside the experience of a court or jury (*R v Loughran* (1999)).

Expert evidence on the 'ultimate issue'

Whether an expert could give his opinion on the ultimate issue, that is, the very question to be decided by the court, was a vexed question for a long time. So far as civil proceedings are concerned, the question is now answered by s 3 of the Civil Evidence Act 1972, which provides that, where a person is called as a witness in civil proceedings, his opinion on any relevant matter, including an issue in the proceedings, shall be admissible if he is qualified to give expert evidence on it.

In criminal cases, evidence of an expert on a particular matter is sometimes excluded on the ground that it would be providing an opinion on the ultimate issue (see, for example, *R v Theodosi* (1993)), but the rule is frequently ignored. Thus, in *R v Stockwell* (1993), the Court of Appeal said that an expert is called to give his opinion and should be allowed to do so. What is important is that the judge should make it clear to the jury that they are not bound by an expert's opinion.

Civil proceedings

Unlike in criminal proceedings (where expert evidence is only admissible if it falls *outside* of the court's experience), Part 35 of the Civil Procedure Rules 1988 (CPR) provides that even where a matter does not fall outside the court's experience, the court is empowered to exclude, restrict or limit the nature of the expert evidence.

Court's permission

Part 35 of the CPR requires the court to restrict expert evidence to that which is reasonably required to resolve the proceedings and accordingly the court's permission is required either to call an expert or to put an expert's report in evidence. Once such permission is given, evidence will normally be given by written report and the parties will not be entitled to call their expert witnesses to give evidence *unless* the court directs that the experts attend the hearing. Where the parties wish to adduce expert evidence in relation to an issue, the court may select a single joint expert from a list that the parties have prepared or approved, or may direct another method of selecting a single joint expert.

Individual experts

Part 35 of the CPR further provides that where a single joint expert is not used, the court will direct the parties to exchange expert reports at the same time on a specified date. If a party fails to disclose an expert's report in accordance with the court's direction, the party will not be able to rely on the report or to call the expert at the trial without the court's permission. A party is entitled to put written questions about the report to the expert within 28 days of its service. The purpose of these questions would be to clarify any issues and the expert's answers would be treated as part of the report. If the expert fails to provide answers to the questions asked, then the court may direct that the party who instructed the expert cannot rely on his evidence.

Note: once disclosed, any party at the trial may use an expert's report.

Additional powers under Part 35 of the CPR

The court may direct one party to provide another party with information (for example, blood test results), which is not otherwise accessible to that other party. Similarly, the court may direct discussions between the experts (in situations where parties have their own experts) in an attempt to identify and agree the expert issues.

Contents of the report

Duty of the expert

Part 35 of the CPR provides that the expert is under a duty to help the court. This duty overrides the expert's duty to the party who instructed him and the understanding and compliance of this duty needs to be reiterated in his report.

Qualifications/instructions/literature/research

The report must specify the expert's qualifications and provide a summary of the expert's instructions. It is also a requirement that the report specifies the literature, research, etc, that the expert has relied on when making the report.

Conclusions

The report must provide the expert's conclusions. If there is a 'range' of views, the report must summarise these and must indicate why the expert arrived at a particular opinion or conclusion.

Statement of truth

A 'statement of truth' must verify the report.

Inaccurate or incomplete report

If there are reasonable grounds to consider that the summary of instructions contained in the expert's report is inaccurate or incomplete, the court may order disclosure of documents or questioning of witnesses in relation to the instructions.

Failure to comply with the requirements of Part 35 of the CPR

If an expert's report does not comply with the requirements of Part 35 of the CPR and/or the expert witness does not appear to have complied with his duty to the court, the court may exclude the expert's evidence.

12 Privilege

This chapter and the next deal with reasons for excluding evidence that are unlike any previously encountered. Other exclusionary rules or principles have as the reason for their existence the need to secure a fair trial. The justification for the rules relating to privilege and public interest immunity has nothing to do with the fairness of the trial but with some other benefit that is thought to be more important. The rules about privilege and public interest immunity acknowledge that the public have interests that must occasionally be allowed to prevail over their interest in securing fair trials, at which all relevant and otherwise admissible evidence can be heard. Although these topics have this understanding in common, they operate differently. A *privilege* is a *right which the law gives to a person* allowing him to refuse to testify about a particular matter or to withhold a document. Effect is given to *public interest immunity* by means of a *power which the courts have* to exclude evidence on the ground that disclosure of information would be damaging to the general good.

There are three main privileges:

- privilege against self-incrimination;

- legal professional privilege;

- privilege arising from statements made 'without prejudice'.

Privilege against self-incrimination

Section 14(1) of the Civil Evidence Act 1968, which is declaratory of the common law (*Rio Tinto Zinc Corp v Westinghouse Electric Corp* (1978)), describes this privilege as the right of a person in any legal proceedings, other than criminal proceedings, to refuse to answer any question or produce any document or thing if to do so would tend to expose that person to proceedings for an offence or for the recovery of a penalty. Section 14 extends the privilege in civil proceedings to protect a person's spouse. At common law, the privilege was restricted to the person claiming it.

The privilege has to be claimed, on oath, by the person who wishes to rely on it. Thus, it cannot be claimed on discovery in a civil action by a solicitor on his client's behalf (*Downie v Coe* (1997)).

Proceedings for civil contempt are proceedings for the 'recovery of a penalty' for the purpose of s 14 of the Civil Evidence Act 1968 (*Cobra Golf v Rata* (1997)). The privilege is available even in respect of the risk of contempt proceedings in the action in which the privilege is claimed (*Memory Corp plc v Sidhu* (2000)).

Statutes have abolished the privilege in certain cases. Sometimes, that has been done by providing that a person may be questioned, but that only a limited use may be made of his answers (see, for example, s 31 of the Theft Act 1968; s 9 of the Criminal Damage Act 1971; s 98 of the Children Act 1989). At one time, it was thought that the scope of the privilege could be cut down by the courts in a similar way, but it is now accepted that where statute has not limited the use to which such evidence can be put, the civil courts have no power to impose a limit of their own devising (*Bishopsgate Investment Management Ltd v Maxwell* (1993)).

As well as cases where the privilege has been expressly removed by statute, there are cases where statutes have impliedly removed it. See, for example, *Re London United Investments plc* (1992) in relation to examinations under s 432 of the Companies Act 1985; *Bank of England v Riley* (1992) in relation to examinations under the Banking Act 1987; *Bishopsgate Investment Management Ltd v Maxwell* (1993) in relation to inquiries under s 235 or 236 of the Insolvency Act 1986.

Article 6 of the European Convention on Human Rights

In certain situations, statute expressly or impliedly removes the privilege against self-incrimination without affording any alternative means of protection. The effect of this is that a person is compelled to provide evidence, which is later used in criminal proceedings against him. This provision is likely to result in a violation of Art 6 of the European Convention on Human Rights (*Saunders v UK* (1996)). In order to avoid future violations of Art 6, a number of these statutory provisions have been amended by the Youth Justice and Criminal Evidence Act 1999. An example of such an amendment can be seen in the examination of persons by the Department of Trade and Industry. Here the prosecution cannot adduce evidence concerning the defendant's answers to inspectors' questions, nor can he be questioned about those answers in subsequent criminal proceedings.

Legal professional privilege

The scope of legal professional privilege at common law is reflected in s 10 of the Police and Criminal Evidence Act 1984 (PACE) (*R v Central Criminal Court ex p Francis and Francis* (1988)). There are three categories set out in the Act.

Section 10(1)(a) of PACE

Deals with communications between a professional legal adviser and his client (or any person representing his client) which are made in connection with the giving of legal advice to the client. Here, the communication is a two-way system and can be thought of in the form of a straight line, with the client or his agent at one end and the legal adviser at the other. Thus:

Client/agent $\longleftrightarrow$ Legal adviser

The legal advice can be of any kind and does not have to be connected with litigation or the prospect of it. The protection is available even where the lawyer is an 'in-house' lawyer advising his employers (*Alfred Crompton Amusement Machines Ltd v Customs & Excise Commissioners* (1972)).

In *Balabel v Air India* (1988), Taylor LJ said that, although the test for a privileged communication was whether it had been made confidentially for the purpose of obtaining legal advice, this purpose was not to be narrowly construed and should be taken to include practical advice about what should be done in the relevant legal context.

Section 10(1)(b) of PACE

Deals with communications between lawyer, client *and third parties* for the purpose of pending or contemplated litigation. The lines of communication can be seen as forming a triangle so as to involve three parties instead of two. Thus:

Third party

Client/agent   Legal adviser

Here, the communications with the third parties, often other professionals such as surveyors, doctors or accountants, will be protected only if the dominant purpose is for use in litigation, pending or contemplated (*Waugh v BRB* (1980)).

Documents obtained for the purpose of obtaining legal advice with respect to pending or contemplated litigation are privileged, even though the litigation is contemplated only by the party seeking the advice, and the other prospective party is unaware that litigation might arise (*Plummers Ltd v Debenhams plc* (1986)).

Section 10(1)(c) of PACE

This covers items enclosed with or referred to in communications of types (a) or (b), provided that the items came into existence in connection with the giving of legal advice and are in the possession of a person who is entitled to possession of them. The point here is that the privilege exists to protect communications between client, legal adviser and, sometimes, third parties. It does not exist to protect evidence from production (*R v King* (1983)).

Copies of original documents are frequently brought into existence in the course of a legal professional relationship. Whether their disclosure can be compelled depends on whether the *originals* would have been privileged or not. If the originals would not, the copies will not attract privilege just because they are part of a set of instructions to enable the client to obtain legal advice (*Dubai Bank v Galadari* (1989)).

Legal professional privilege will not protect a communication to facilitate crime or fraud (*R v Cox and Railton* (1884); s 10(2) of PACE). 'Fraud' is very widely defined to include, in addition to the tort of deceit, 'all forms of fraud and dishonesty such as fraudulent breach of contract, fraudulent conspiracy, trickery and sham contrivances' (*Crescent Farm (Sidcup) Sports Ltd v Sterling Offices Ltd* (1972), *per* Goff J). This exception to the scope of legal professional privilege has more recently been expressed by saying that, for the privilege to apply, there must be 'absence of iniquity' (*Ventouris v Mountain* (1991), *per* Bingham LJ). In *Barclays Bank v Eustice* (1995), 'iniquity' was held to include obtaining advice about how to structure a series of transactions at an undervalue that would have had the effect of prejudicing the interests of creditors. The Court of Appeal held that it made no difference that neither the solicitor nor even the client realised that this would be the effect of what was proposed.

Criminal or fraudulent conduct undertaken by investigative agents employed by solicitors in the conduct of litigation will also cause the privilege to be lost (*Dubai Aluminium Co Ltd v Al Alawi* (1999)).

Experts' reports that are to be used at trial will have to be disclosed to the other party but one party may obtain a report that he later decides not to use. Such a report will normally be covered by legal professional privilege. However, there are two exceptions to this rule:

- reports from experts, such as doctors and psychiatrists, brought into existence by parties to cases involving the welfare of children. The overriding duty to regard the welfare of a child as paramount in such cases will not allow the parties to suppress 'unfavourable' reports (*Oxfordshire CC v M* (1994));

- where an expert in his report refers to material that was supplied to him for the purpose of obtaining his opinion, any privilege attaching to that material will be waived when the expert's report is served on the other party. It makes no difference that the expert might have found the material unhelpful or irrelevant (*Clough v Tameside and Glossop HA* (1998)).

Duration of privilege

The general rule is, 'Once privileged, always privileged' (*Calcraft v Guest* (1898), *per* Lindley MR). So, documents prepared for one action will continue to be privileged in subsequent litigation, even though the subject matter or the parties may be different. See, for example, *The Aegis Blaze* (1986). Another example of the maxim is the rule whereby documents concerning property rights that are privileged in the hands of one owner are privileged in the hands of that person's successors in title (*Minet v Morgan* (1873)).

Privilege

Legal professional privilege

It used to be thought that, where the holder of a privilege could derive no further benefit from its exercise, the privilege could be defeated by the interest of another person who needed to have access to the information, particularly where this was needed to defeat a criminal charge. However, since the decision of the House of Lords in *R v Derby Magistrates ex p B* (1995), it is clear that this is not the case. The House of Lords said there that earlier decisions to the contrary had been wrong. It is a fundamental condition, on which the administration of justice rests, that a client must be sure that what he tells his lawyer will never be revealed without consent. Otherwise, the client might hold back half the truth.

Does the privilege apply to all parties and to all types of communications?

In relation to communications between a party to negotiations and a third party, the privilege only applies to admissions (*Murrell v Healey* (2001)). However, in respect of the parties to the negotiations, the privilege applies to all communications between the parties and not merely to admissions (*Unilever plc v Proctor & Gamble* (1999)).

Bypassing the privilege via secondary evidence

Legal professional privilege prevents facts *from having to be disclosed*. It does not prevent the facts *from being proved* if any other means of doing so can be found. Thus, in *Calcraft v Guest* (1898), where the appellant had obtained copies of certain privileged documents and so was in a position to prove the contents of the originals by means of secondary evidence, the Court of Appeal held that he was entitled to do so.

In civil proceedings, r 31.20 of the Civil Procedure Rules 1998 (CPR) provides that 'inadvertently disclosed privileged documents may only be used with the consent of the court'. It is likely that courts will be guided by earlier decisions in cases where the use of privileged documents was restrained by injunction, so some knowledge of earlier decisions will be helpful. In particular, it was held before the CPR came into force that, where a privileged document had been inadvertently disclosed, the privilege would not be lost if a reasonable person seeing it would have realised that it could only have been disclosed in error (see also *Pizzey v Ford Motor Co Ltd* (1993); *IBM Corp v Phoenix (International) Computers Ltd* (1995)). Where a privileged document has been disclosed by misconduct, or has been obtained by malpractice, the old law presumably applies. It will be necessary to obtain an injunction (albeit in the same proceedings) restraining the use of that document. In the leading case that established this right, *Ashburton v Pape* (1913), the injunction was granted on the basis of the court's power to protect confidentiality. However, in *Goddard v Nationwide Building Society* (1986), Nourse LJ took the view that the basis of the relief was not the confidential nature of the communication, but the legal professional privilege attached to it. The importance of this distinction may lie in the fact that, on the more recent view, there appears to be less scope for a judge to exercise his discretion when deciding whether to grant the injunction (*Derby and Co Ltd v Weldon (No 8)* (1990)).

In *Butler v Board of Trade* (1971), it was held that public policy would prevent an injunction of this kind from being granted where its effect would be to restrain the prosecution from adducing admissible evidence in criminal proceedings and, in a case where the prosecution obtained a privileged communication by accident rather than impropriety, the Court of Appeal held that it could be used during the cross-examination of the defendant (*R v Tompkins* (1977)).

'Without prejudice' statements

This head of privilege is founded on the public policy of encouraging litigants to settle their differences. The rule applies to exclude from evidence all negotiations genuinely aimed at settlement, whether oral or in writing. Such statements are 'without prejudice' to their makers if the terms proposed are not accepted. The application of the rule does not depend on the use of the expression 'without prejudice', though it is safer to use it. If the circumstances make it clear that the parties were trying to settle a claim, evidence of the negotiations will not generally be admissible to establish an admission. Conversely, the use of the 'without prejudice' label will be of no effect where there is no attempt at settlement (*Re Daintrey ex p Holt* (1893)).

Evidence of negotiations will be admissible if it is necessary to show the terms of a settlement that were ultimately reached: for example, where one of the parties wants to sue on that agreement (*Tomlin v Standard Telephones and Cables Ltd* (1969)), but, generally, the 'without prejudice' rule makes evidence of negotiations inadmissible in any subsequent litigation connected with the same subject matter, even where the parties are not identical (*Rush & Tomkins Ltd v GLC* (1989)).

13 Public interest immunity

Public interest immunity (PII), formerly called 'Crown privilege', is a rule of law that requires the withholding of documents on the ground that it would be harmful to the public interest to disclose them.

In *Duncan v Cammell Laird and Co Ltd* (1942), the House of Lords held that a court could not question a claim of Crown privilege, if made in proper form. It also said that claims to Crown privilege could be put on two alternative grounds:

- disclosure of the contents of the particular documents would harm the public interest, for example, by endangering national security or prejudicing diplomatic relations;

- the documents belonged to a class of documents that had to be withheld in the interests of 'the proper functioning of the public service'.

130

In 1956, Viscount Kilmuir LC, in a statement in the House of Lords, explained that the reason for claiming Crown privilege on a class, as opposed to a contents, basis was that it was needed to secure 'freedom and candour of communications with and within the public service', so that government decisions could be taken on the best advice and with the fullest information. People advising the Government must be able to know that they were doing so in confidence and that any document containing their advice would not subsequently be disclosed.

The beginning of the modern approach to PII can be seen in *Conway v Rimmer* (1968), in which the House of Lords reversed its earlier ruling in *Duncan v Cammell Laird* and held that, in such cases, it was for the court to decide where the balance of public interest lay: in protecting a government claim for secrecy or in upholding a litigant's right to have all relevant materials available for the proper adjudication of his claim. However, the idea that PII might be based on a class, rather than a contents, claim was still accepted.

PII can operate in cases not involving the Government. In
R v Lewes JJ ex p Secretary of State for the Home Department
(1973), it was said that the old expression, 'Crown privilege',
was wrong and misleading. While a minister was always an
appropriate, and often the most appropriate, person to assert
the public interest, it was open to any person to raise the issue,
and there might be cases where the trial judge himself should
do so. So, for example, in *D v NSPCC* (1978), the House of
Lords protected the anonymity of an informer who had reported
suspicions of child cruelty to the NSPCC.

An important distinction between PII and the sort of privilege
that might be claimed by a private litigant, such as legal
professional privilege or the privilege against self-incrimination,
used to be that a privilege might be waived but a claim to PII
could not (see, for example, *Makanjuola v Commissioner of
Metropolitan Police* (1992), *per* Bingham LJ). This approach,
coupled with a class claim rather than a contents claim, led to
undesirably wide PII claims being made by ministers in a
number of trials. The practice was criticised in the Scott Report
(1996) and the Government has now effectively abandoned
class claims. In *R v Chief Constable of West Midlands ex p
Wiley* (1995), the House of Lords held that a class claim cannot
be made in respect of documents compiled as part of the
investigation of a complaint against the police.

In recent decades, the leading cases on PII in the House of
Lords have been concerned with civil claims and it is unclear
whether the principles expressed in them are equally applicable
in criminal trials, but it is clear that PII does apply in criminal
trials (see ss 3(6) and 7(5) of the **Criminal Procedure and
Investigations Act 1996**).

The basic rule is that, in public prosecutions, witnesses may not
be asked, and will not be allowed to disclose, the names of
informers or the nature of the information given. The reason for
the rule is that informers need to be protected, both for their

own safety and to ensure that the supply of information about criminal activities does not dry up (*Marks v Beyfus* (1890)). This rule can be departed from if the disclosure of the name of the informant was necessary to show the defendant's innocence, but it is for the defendant to show that there is a good reason for disclosure (*R v Hennessey* (1978)).

The rule in *Marks v Beyfus* also protects the identity of persons who have allowed their premises to be used for police observation, as well as the identity of the premises from which observation was kept. Even if the defendant argues that identification of the premises is necessary to establish his innocence (because, for example, it has a bearing on the accuracy of witness observations), the judge may still refuse to allow the question to be put (*R v Johnson* (1989)). The prosecution must first provide a proper evidential basis to support their claim for protection of identity. In *R v Johnson*, Watkins LJ stated the following as minimum requirements:

- the police officer in charge of the observations must testify that he visited all the observation places to be used and ascertained the attitude of their occupiers, both as to the use to be made of them and to possible subsequent disclosure;

- a police officer of at least the rank of chief inspector must testify that, immediately prior to the trial, he visited the places used for observation and ascertained whether the occupiers were the same as when the observation took place and, whether they were or not, the attitude of those occupiers to possible disclosure of their premises as observation points.

The object of keeping the identity of premises secret is to protect the owner or occupier. Where this consideration does not apply, cross-examination may be permitted on the details of surveillance (*R v Brown* (1987)).

A police informer may voluntarily sacrifice his anonymity, and PII cannot be used to prevent this (*Savage v Chief Constable of Hampshire* (1997)).

Crown Court (Criminal Procedure and Investigations Act 1996) (Disclosure) Rules 1997

The prosecution may seek to claim public interest immunity at an *ex parte* hearing without notifying the defence. This is appropriate where the fact that an application is being made would in itself reveal to the defence the information to which the public interest immunity claim relates. The prosecution may seek to claim public interest immunity at an *ex parte* hearing, having notified the defence that an application is being made. This procedure is appropriate where revealing the nature of the relevant material would reveal to the defence the information to which the public interest immunity claim relates. Or finally, the prosecution may seek to claim public interest immunity at an *inter partes* hearing, having notified the defence of the nature of the material. Note, however, where the prosecution seeks to claim public interest immunity by way of one of the procedures described above, the court can direct the prosecution to adopt an alternative procedure.

14 Facts not requiring proof

The general rule is that, if a party wants to rely on a particular fact in support of his case, that fact must be formally proved by providing evidence of it at trial. To this rule there are two important exceptions:

- formal admissions; and
- judicial notice.

Formal admissions

Civil trials

By r 14.1 of the Civil Procedure Rules 1998 (CPR), a party may admit the truth of the whole or any part of another party's case. He may do this by giving notice in writing, for example, in a statement of case or by letter.

A notice to admit facts may be served under r 32.18 of the CPR. Such a notice must be served no later than 21 days before the trial. Where the other party makes any admission in response to the notice, the admission may be used against him only:

- in the proceedings in which the notice is served; and
- by the party who served the notice.

Criminal trials

By s 10(1) of the Criminal Justice Act 1967:

- any fact of which oral evidence may be given in any criminal proceedings may be admitted for the purpose of those proceedings by or on behalf of the prosecutor or defendant;
- the admission of any such fact shall, as against the party making the admission, be conclusive evidence in those proceedings of the fact admitted.

By s 10(2), an admission under s 10(1) may be made before or at the proceedings, but, if made otherwise than in court, it must be in writing.

By s 10(3), an admission under this section for the purpose of proceedings relating to any matter shall be treated as an admission for the purpose of any subsequent criminal proceedings relating to that matter (including any appeal or retrial).

By s 10(4), an admission under this section may with the leave of the court be withdrawn in the proceedings for the purpose of which it is made or any subsequent criminal proceedings relating to the same matter.

A *Practice Direction* of 1995 provides that where there is a plea of not guilty at a plea and directions hearing, both prosecution and defence are expected to inform the court of facts which are to be admitted and which can be reduced into writing under s 10(2).

Judicial notice

'Judicial notice' refers to the acceptance by a judicial tribunal of the truth of a fact without formal proof, on the ground that it is within the knowledge of the tribunal itself.

Judicial notice may be applied to facts, which a judge can be called upon to accept:

- from his general knowledge of them (facts judicially noticed 'without inquiry');
- from inquiries to be made by him for his own information from sources to which it is proper for him to refer (facts judicially noticed 'after inquiry');
- by virtue of some statutory provision.

Facts judicially noticed without inquiry

These are facts that are regarded as matters of common knowledge. For example, in recent decades, courts have taken judicial notice of the following facts:

- stripes are often used in football shirts to identify various teams (*Cook and Hurst's Design Application* (1979));

- Elvis Presley lived in the US (*RCA Corp v Pollard* (1982));

- postmen leave notices to the effect that a recorded delivery letter is being held for collection (*Hussein v Secretary of State for the Environment* (1984));

- temperatures fall at night (*Watts v Reigate and Banstead BC* (1984));

- more men than women leave surviving spouses (*Turner v The Labour Party* (1987));

- clearing banks in the UK usually charge compound, rather than simple, interest (*Bello v Barclays Bank plc* (1994));

- risky investments usually attract much higher rates of return than those with little risk attached (*IRC v Universities Superannuation Scheme Ltd* (1997)).

138 What is common knowledge differs according to time and place. For example, in *Calabar (Woolwich) Ltd v Tesco Stores* (1977), the Court of Appeal took the view that supermarkets were a recent and still growing development, and that courts could not take judicial notice of facts about them, but needed evidence.

Facts judicially noticed after inquiry

Whenever the meaning of words arises, however technical or obscure, then, unless there is some dispute about it, it is common practice for the court to inform itself by any means that are reliable and ready to hand. Counsel usually give any necessary explanation, or reference may be made to a dictionary (*Baldwin and Francis Ltd v Patents Appeal Tribunal* (1959)).

For the purposes of more complicated inquiries, reference may be made to such sources as reports of earlier cases, certificates from responsible officials, letters from Secretaries of State or statements made in court by counsel on their behalf, works of reference and the oral statements of witnesses. The cases show that such inquiries have generally been made in at least three types of case:

- where information is required about current political or diplomatic matters;

- where information is required about historical facts;

- where information is required about customs, including professional practices.

Current political and diplomatic matters

If a court needs information about matters of this kind, it may formally ask a government minister to provide it. The answer will be regarded as conclusive in relation to the matters with which it deals (*Duff Development Co Ltd v Government of Kelantan* (1924)). Judicial notice has been used in determining:

- whether a foreign country was a sovereign independent State (*Duff Development Co Ltd v Government of Kelantan* (1924));

- the extent of the UK monarch's territorial sovereignty (*The Fagernes* (1927));

- whether a person was entitled to diplomatic immunity (*Engelke v Musman* (1928));

- whether a state of war existed between the UK and a foreign State (*R v Bottrill ex p Kuechenmeister* (1947)).

Historical facts

It was held by the Judicial Committee of the Privy Council in *Read v Bishop of Lincoln* (1892) that, when it is important to ascertain 'ancient facts of a public nature', the law permits historical works to be referred to.

The view was formerly taken that, while judicial notice might be taken of facts of this nature, it would not extend to historical facts of a contemporary, or nearly contemporary, kind. See, for example, *Commonwealth Shipping Representative v P & O Branch Service* (1923). However, more recent decisions suggest that judicial knowledge may be taken of contemporary, or near contemporary, events. For example, judicial notice has been taken that:

- the invasion of Holland by the German army was in full swing during working hours on 10 May 1940 (*Cornelius v Banque Franco-Serbe* (1941));

- the American declaration of war against Japan took place in December 1941 and American forces began to arrive in the UK in working parties in 1942 (*R v Birkenhead Borough JJ ex p Smith* (1954));

- the Katyn massacre occurred (*Re St Luke's Chelsea* (1976));

- 1975 was an inflationary period when, in general, land values were rising rapidly (*Washington Development Corp v Bamblings (Washington) Ltd* (1984));

- house sales and housing development were declining rapidly in England during 1990–92 (*Bovis Homes Ltd v Oakcliff Investment Corp* (1994));

- there was currently religious conflict between Sikhs and Hindus in the Punjab (*Sandhu v Sandhu* (1986));

- there was currently a very turbulent political situation in Hebron (*Re A-R* (1997)).

Customs

Judicial notice may be taken of general customs that have been proved in earlier cases, despite the general rule that a court cannot treat a fact as proved on the basis of evidence heard in a previous case (*George v Davies* (1911)).

Judicial notice may also be taken of customs as a matter of general knowledge. For example, judicial notice has been taken of:

- the practice of the Ordnance Survey Office in compiling Ordnance Survey maps (*Davey v Harrow Corp* (1958));

- the practice of the Comptroller General's Office in relation to applications for patents (*Alliance Flooring Co Ltd v Winsorflor Ltd* (1961));

- the practice of London solicitors in relation to company searches (*Re Garton (Western) Ltd* (1989)).

Statutory provisions

Several Acts of Parliament direct the courts to take judicial notice of various matters. For example:

- the Interpretation Act 1978 provides (re-enacting earlier provisions) that every Act passed after 1850 shall be a public Act and judicially noticed as such unless the contrary is expressly provided;

- by s 3(2) of the European Communities Act 1972, judicial notice is to be taken of various treaties, of the Official Journal of the Communities and of any decision of, or expression of opinion by, the European Court on questions concerning the meaning or effect of any of the treaties or Community instruments.

There is no express provision for taking judicial notice of statutory instruments, but some have been so frequently relied on that judicial notice will be taken of them (*R v Jones* (1969)).

Use of personal knowledge

While it seems clear that a tribunal may make use of its *general* knowledge by virtue of judicial notice, it is also said that neither judges nor jurors can make use of their purely personal knowledge in reaching a decision.

But the Divisional Court has, on several occasions, held that *magistrates* have properly applied their own knowledge of local conditions (*Ingram v Percival* (1969); *Paul v DPP* (1990)).

In *Wetherall v Harrison* (1976), the Divisional Court emphasised that, although such special knowledge could be used to *interpret* the evidence given in court, it must not be used to *contradict* it. In *Bowman v DPP* (1990), it was said that justices must be extremely circumspect in using their own local knowledge. They should inform the parties if they are likely to use such knowledge, so as to give an opportunity for comment on the knowledge that they claim to have.

15 Judicial findings as evidence

The rule at common law is that a judicial finding in one case is inadmissible in another case between different parties to prove the facts on which the first decision was based. The reason for this is that it would be unjust for someone to have his rights affected by litigation to which he was not a party and in which, therefore, he could not be heard (*Duchess of Kingston's case* (1776)). However, this principle was applied in such a way that criminal convictions had to be ignored in cases where common sense would have acknowledged them to be both relevant and weighty. Reform in civil cases was achieved by statute in 1968 and in criminal cases in 1984.

Convictions as evidence in civil cases

At common law, the effect of the rule in *Hollington v Hewthorn* (1943) was that, in a civil trial, an earlier criminal conviction arising from the same facts was irrelevant and, therefore, inadmissible.

The position was changed by the Civil Evidence Act 1968. By s 11(1), in any civil proceedings, the fact that a person has been convicted of an offence by a UK court, or by a court martial in the UK or elsewhere, shall be admissible in evidence for the purpose of proving, where to do so is relevant to any issue in those proceedings, that he committed that offence.

By s 11(2), where a person is proved to have been convicted of an offence he shall be taken to have committed that offence unless the contrary is proved. But, by s 13(1), in an action for libel or slander in which the question of whether a person did or did not commit a criminal offence is relevant to an issue arising in the action, proof of the conviction is conclusive evidence that the person convicted committed that offence.

Because s 11(1) refers only to UK convictions, the rule in *Hollington v Hewthorn* (1943) continues to apply to convictions by foreign courts and they therefore remain irrelevant and inadmissible (*Union Carbide Corp v Naturin Ltd* (1987)). Nor does the section extend to adjudications of guilt in police disciplinary proceedings (*Thorpe v Chief Constable of Greater Manchester* (1989)).

If a person has been convicted but there is an appeal pending, the court will not rely on the section. Instead, the civil hearing will be adjourned until the criminal appeal has been determined (*Re Raphael (Dec'd)* (1973)).

The effect of s 11

There are two views about the effect of the section:

● the conviction itself has no weight as an item of evidence, but operates only as a trigger to activate the presumption under s 11(2) that the facts on which it was based are true;

● the conviction is in itself an item of evidence to be weighed in the scales against the defendant.

Both views can be found in the judgments of the Court of Appeal in *Stupple v Royal Insurance Co Ltd* (1971). Support for the second view can be found in *Hunter v Chief Constable of West Midlands* (1982).

Convictions as evidence in criminal cases

Some offences presuppose the commission of an earlier offence by someone else; for example, handling presupposes that the property handled has already been stolen. However, at common law, the earlier offence could not be proved by showing that someone had been convicted of it. The earlier conviction was regarded as no more than non-expert evidence of opinion and so inadmissible (*R v Turner* (1832)). The law is now governed by s 74 of the Police and Criminal Evidence Act 1984 (PACE).

Section 74 of PACE

By sub-s (1), in any proceedings, the fact that a person other than the accused has been convicted of an offence by any court in the UK shall be admissible in evidence for the purpose of proving, where to do so is relevant to any issue in those proceedings, that that person committed that offence.

By sub-s (2), where such evidence is adduced, that person shall be taken to have committed that offence unless the contrary is proved. Proof is to the civil standard, because that is the standard always applied where a defendant in a criminal case has the burden of proof in respect of any issue (*R v Carr-Briant* (1943)).

The scope of s 74(1)

Clearly, proof of the commission of an earlier offence will be 'relevant to any issue' in the current proceedings if it establishes an element of the offence now charged. So, for example, in *R v Pigram* (1995), where two men were charged with handling stolen goods, the plea of guilty made by one of the defendants was held admissible at the trial of the other for the purpose of proving that the goods were stolen.

The Court of Appeal has held that a wide interpretation should be applied to 'issue' so as to allow it to cover not just essential ingredients of an offence, but evidentiary matters also. In *R v Castle* (1989), evidence of the previous conviction, on his own plea of guilty, of someone who was no longer a defendant in the trial was held admissible to support a prosecution witness' evidence of identification.

While the Court of Appeal has said that it does not approve of allowing evidence to go before a jury that is irrelevant, inadmissible, prejudicial or unfair simply on the basis that it is convenient for the jury to have 'the whole picture' (*R v Boyson* (1991)), it has also been said that 'anything which enables a jury better to understand the relevant factual background against which the issue arises is properly to be described as relevant to that issue within the terms of s 74'. So, in a case where defendants were charged with conspiracy to pervert the course of justice by obtaining the false evidence of witnesses at an earlier trial, it was held proper to have proved that the earlier trial had resulted in a conviction, and that at a later trial others had already been convicted of conspiracy to pervert the course of justice in relation to the earlier trial (*R v Buckingham* (1993)). In *R v Warner* (1992), the defendants were charged with conspiracy to supply heroin. The prosecution case was based in part on police observations at the address of one of the defendants. These revealed that a great many people had visited the house. Eight of the visitors observed by the police had previous convictions for the possession or supply of heroin. The trial judge allowed evidence of these convictions to be adduced under s 74 and was upheld by the Court of Appeal. The previous convictions of the visitors were relevant to the characters of the people that the defendants were letting into the house and this had a bearing on the nature of the transactions going on there.

Interaction with s 78(1)

Once a judge is satisfied that the evidence tendered under s 74(1) has some probative force, careful consideration should be given to s 78(1) to see whether the discretion to exclude should be exercised (*R v Boyson* (1991)).

In several cases (for example, *R v Kempster* (1989)), the Court of Appeal has suggested that the discretion to exclude ought to be exercised where the earlier conviction was obtained as the result of a guilty plea, rather than a contested trial. But the court has not always taken this view. See, for example, *R v Grey* (1988) and *R v Turner* (1991).

It has been said that the sub-section should be 'sparingly' used (*R v Robertson* (1987); *R v Stewart* (1999)) and, in *Warner v Jones* (1988), it was suggested that it might have been wiser not to use it since it added little to an already strong case against the defendants.

It has also been said that, where the evidence that the prosecution wishes to adduce under s 74(1) expressly or by

Judicial findings

Convictions as evidence

necessary inference imports the complicity of the person on trial in the offence with which he is charged, the sub-section should not be used (*R v Kempster* (1989)). The cases on conspiracy show that in that area this principle is likely to be applied.

In *R v O'Connor* (1987), a case in which conspiracy between only two persons was alleged, the Court of Appeal held that the trial judge should have used s 78(1) to exclude evidence of the co-accused's conviction (see also *R v Robertson* (1987), where the conspiracy was alleged to have been between the defendant, two other named men, and other unknown persons. The Court of Appeal held that evidence of the convictions of the other named men had been rightly admitted).

16 Documentary evidence

A party who wishes to rely on a statement contained in a document as evidence supporting his case needs to consider, in addition to any other relevant evidence law, at least one further matter: proof of the contents of the document. In some cases, proof of due execution may have to be considered also.

Proving statements contained in documents in criminal proceedings

Section 133 of the Criminal Justice Act 2003 provides that where a statement in a document is admissible as evidence in criminal proceedings, the statement may be proved by producing either:

- the document; or
- (whether or not the document exists) a copy of the document or of the material part of it, authenticated in whatever way the court may approve.

Unavailable document

In criminal proceedings, the admissibility of oral evidence of the contents of a document is governed by common law. The basic common law rule is that only primary evidence of the contents of a document (that is, the original document itself) is admissible. There are three relevant exceptions:

- *Destruction or loss of original*
  Destruction by fire was one of the earliest acceptable excuses for failure to produce an original (*Leyfield's case* (1611)), and the principle was afterwards extended to cover other circumstances in which the original had been lost or destroyed (*Blackie v Pidding* (1848)). Before the exception can be applied where a document is missing, proof must be given that an adequate search has been made (*Brewster v Sewell* (1820)).

- *Other impossibility or inconvenience*
  Production of a document may be excused, and secondary evidence given of its contents, when it is impossible for reasons other than destruction or loss to produce it, or even when it would be highly inconvenient to do so. Thus, secondary evidence can be admitted of writing on a wall and of an inscription on a tombstone (*Mortimer v M'Callan* (1840)). Similarly, secondary evidence has been admitted of:

  - inscriptions on flags and banners (*R v Hunt* (1820));
  - the contents of a placard on a wall (*Bruce v Nicolopulo* (1855));
  - the contents of a document in the custody of a foreign court (*Alivon v Furnival* (1834));
  - the contents of a notice that was required by statute to be fixed permanently to a wall (*Owner v Bee Hive Spinning Co Ltd* (1914));
  - the contents of a computer disk on which information was stored (*R v Nazeer* (1998)).

- *Lawful non-production by a stranger*
  Secondary evidence will be admissible where a stranger to the litigation lawfully declines to produce a document in his possession or control. (A witness with no such justification can, in theory, be compelled to produce a document at trial by a witness summons.) Thus, secondary evidence has been given of the contents of a document where:

  - the original was unavailable because of privilege (*Mills v Oddy* (1834));
  - the document was in the possession of a stranger outside the jurisdiction (*Kilgour v Owen* (1889));
  - the document was in the possession of a person entitled to diplomatic immunity (*R v Nowaz* (1976)).

The party who adduces a document in evidence must usually, in the absence of an admission by his opponent, prove that it was duly executed. This obligation may simply require evidence that the document was signed by the person whose signature it purports to bear. Sometimes, it may be necessary to prove the handwriting of the whole of a disputed document. Proof of execution may also require proof of attestation.

Proof of a signature or of handwriting may be made in one or more of the following ways:

- by evidence of the writer, or of someone else who saw the maker of the document write it or put his signature on it;

- by evidence of opinion given by an ordinary witness. Such evidence is admissible even where the evidence of the writer is available. Thus, on a charge of forgery, it is not *necessary* to call the person whose signature is alleged to have been forged (*R v Hurley* (1843));

- by an actual comparison, often aided by expert opinion evidence. Section 8 of the Criminal Procedure Act 1865 applies to both civil and criminal proceedings and provides that comparison of a disputed writing with any writing proved to the satisfaction of the judge to be genuine shall be permitted to be made by witnesses; and such writings, and the evidence of witnesses respecting the same, may be submitted to the court and jury as evidence of the genuineness or otherwise of the writing in dispute.

In civil proceedings, the judge has to be satisfied on the balance of probabilities as to the genuineness of the writing that is to be used as a standard for comparison. In criminal proceedings, he must be satisfied beyond reasonable doubt (*R v Ewing* (1983)).

The Criminal Procedure Act 1865 does not expressly *require* the evidence of witnesses. Once a document has been proved to the judge's satisfaction to be a genuine sample of handwriting from the person who is alleged to have written the disputed document, it may simply be compared with the disputed document by the jury. But it has been held that, in criminal cases, expert evidence should also be available (*R v Harden* (1963)).

'Attestation' refers to the signature of a document by a person who is not a party to it, but who is a witness to the signature of one of the parties. By s 3 of the Evidence Act 1938, any document required by law to be attested, with the exception of a will or other testamentary document, 'may, instead of being approved by an attesting witness, be proved in the manner in which it might be proved if no attesting witness were alive'. The effect of this provision is that non-testamentary documents required by law to be attested may now be proved by showing that the signature is in fact that of the attesting witness.

Where the court is asked to pronounce for a will in solemn form, the general practice is for at least one of the attesting witnesses to be called to give evidence of execution, but a will can be pronounced for where both attesting witnesses are proved to be dead, or even if the evidence shows merely that they cannot be traced, if the court is satisfied in all the circumstances that the will was duly executed (*Re Lemon's Estate* (1961)).

In any proceedings, proof of execution may be dispensed with in the case of 'ancient documents', which, by s 4 of the Evidence Act 1938, are documents which are more than 20 years old. For this rule to apply, the document must appear to be regular on the face of it, and must be produced from proper custody. 'Proper custody' is any custody that is consistent with the genuineness and legitimate origin of the document (*Bishop of Meath v Marquess of Winchester* (1836)).

Representation other than by a person

Section 129 of the Criminal Justice Act 2003 provides that where a *representation* of any fact is made otherwise than by a person, but depends for its accuracy on information supplied (directly or indirectly) by a person, the representation is not admissible in criminal proceedings as evidence of the fact, unless it was proved that the information was accurate. Note, however, that this section does not affect the operation of the presumption that the mechanical device has been properly calibrated.

Representation

Section 115 of the Criminal Justice Act 2003 provides that a statement is any representation of fact or opinion made by a person by whatever means and it includes a representation made in a sketch, photofit or other pictorial form. Thus, a representation of fact by a machine, rather than a person, cannot be a hearsay statement. A matter stated is where the purpose or one of the purposes of the person making the statement is to cause another person to believe the matter or to cause another person to act or a machine to operate on the basis that the matter is as stated (s 115(3)). Thus, 'implied assertions' will not be hearsay statements if the person who made them did not have either of these purposes.

Proving statements contained in documents in civil proceedings

Section 8 of the Civil Evidence Act 1995 provides that statements (provided they are admissible in evidence) contained in documents may be proved either by producing the original documents or by producing copies of the documents/relevant parts of the document authenticated in a manner approved by the court. Note also that a copy need not be directly copied from the original document but may be a copy of a copy and it is irrelevant how many levels of copying there are between the original document and the copy. Note also where an original document is not readily available to a party, the party may be permitted to prove its contents at common law by relying on oral evidence of a witness who read the document (*Masquerade Music v Springsteen* (2001)).

Section 9 of the Civil Evidence Act 1995 further provides that it is not necessary to call witnesses/adduce evidence to prove documents which are certified to form part of business or public authority records. However, where appropriate, the court may direct that the provisions of s 9 do not apply to particular documents or types of document.

Exclusionary discretion

Under r 32.1 of the Civil Procedure Rules (CPR) the civil courts possess discretion to exclude evidence that would otherwise be admissible. The court may also give directions in relation to the issues for which it requires evidence and the type of evidence it requires. The court may also give directions as to how such evidence be presented to the court and, where appropriate, may limit the cross-examination of witnesses.

Unavailable document

155

Documentary evidence

17 Real evidence

'Real evidence' is an ill-defined concept. There is general agreement that it includes physical objects produced for the inspection of the court. If a document is adduced in evidence, the question of whether it is 'real' or 'documentary' evidence depends on the purpose for which it is adduced. If the purpose is to establish its contents, it is classed as an item of documentary evidence; if the purpose is to establish its condition or appearance, it is classed as an item of real evidence. 'Real evidence' has also been held to include the following items.

Physical appearance of a person or animal in court

In *Line v Taylor* (1862), a dog was brought into court to display its good temper. Before defendants in criminal trials are allowed to give evidence, the jury might take into account their reactions in the dock at various stages of the trial (*AG for New South Wales v Bertrand* (1867)). The demeanour of a witness has traditionally been regarded as relevant to credibility (*Teper v R* (1952)). The resemblance of a child, produced to the court, to a person alleged to be its father has been held to be some evidence of parentage (*C v C and C* (1972)).

Views

Things and places outside court may be inspected during the course of a trial. In *Buckingham v Daily News Ltd* (1956), the Court of Appeal held that such an inspection was part of the evidence in the case. The parties, their legal representatives and the judge (or judge and jury) should all be present at the view (*R v Ely JJ ex p Burgess* (1992)).

Automatic recordings

Where the recording device operates as no more than a calculator, the printout or other reading is an item of real evidence; for example, the printout produced by a breathalyser (*Castle v Cross* (1984)). In *R v Spiby* (1990), the Court of Appeal had to consider whether the rule against hearsay applied to the printout from a device which monitored telephone calls and recorded the numbers to which calls were made and their duration. The court held that the printout was an item of real evidence and not caught by the hearsay rule, because the recording was entirely automatic and did not depend on anything that had passed through a human mind.

The contents of tape recordings may be admitted as evidence of what was said on a particular occasion (*R v Maqsud Ali* (1966)).

The voices recorded must be identified by admissible evidence, but it is enough merely to establish a *prima facie* case for authenticity (*R v Robson and Harris* (1972)). Such a recording is a document within the meaning of s 27 of the Criminal Justice Act 1988, and a transcript of the recording will be admissible as a copy under the same section.

In *R v Rampling* (1987), the Court of Appeal gave the following guidance on the use in court of tape recordings of police interviews:

- the tape can be produced and proved by the interviewing officer or any other officer present when it was taken;

- the officer should have listened to the tape before the trial so that he can, if necessary, deal with any objections to authenticity or accuracy;

- the transcript of the recording can be produced by the officer. He should have checked this against the recording for accuracy before the trial;

- the defendant is entitled to have any part of the tape played to the jury;

- if any part of the tape is played, it is for the judge to decide whether the jury should have a transcript to enable them to follow the recording more clearly.

159

Real evidence

Subject to any necessary editing to remove inadmissible evidence, a jury in retirement may, on request, be allowed to hear a tape recording of a police interview with the defendant, where the tape has been made an exhibit, even though the tape has not been played earlier during the trial (*R v Riaz and Burke* (1991)). Any playing of the tape after the jury has retired should be in open court, with judge, counsel and the defendant present (*R v Hagan* (1997)).

A jury may also want to see a video tape of an interview with a child once again after retirement. It is a matter for the judge's discretion whether this should happen. If there is a replay, the following rules apply (see *R v Rawlings and Broadbent* (1995)):

- it must be in court, with judge, counsel and defendant present;

- the judge should warn the jury that, because they are hearing the evidence-in-chief of the complainant for a second time, well after all the other evidence, they should guard against the risk of giving it disproportionate weight simply for that reason, and should bear well in mind the other evidence in the case;

- to assist in maintaining a fair balance, when the video has been replayed, the judge should remind the jury from his own notes of the cross-examination and reexamination of the complainant, whether the jury ask him to do so or not.

In *R v Morris* (1998), the Court of Appeal said that the transcript of a child's evidence-in-chief, given by way of video interview, should only rarely remain with the jury when they have retired to consider their verdict. In those rare cases, the judge must warn the jury against giving it disproportionate weight.

A film or photograph may be admitted to prove the commission of an offence and the identity of the offender. For example, in *R v Dodson* (1984), photographs taken by a security camera at a building society office were held admissible to show an offence being committed. Films or photographs are treated as if they are extensions of human perception. In *Taylor v Chief Constable of Cheshire* (1986), police officers saw a video recording made by a security camera of someone picking up an item in a shop and putting it in his jacket. The police identified the man as the defendant. The film was later accidentally erased, but the Court of Appeal held that the officers' evidence of what they had seen on the tape had been properly admitted because they were in effect in the position of bystanders who had witnessed the event.

161

Real evidence

18 Estoppel

Statement of the rule

An 'estoppel' exists when, in consequence of some previous act or statement to which he is a party, a person is precluded from afterwards showing the existence of a different state of affairs than that indicated by the previous act or statement.

The rule is based on considerations of justice and public policy. It would be *unjust* to allow someone to do or say something, yet afterwards try to obtain an advantage by denying the validity of what he did earlier, or the truth of what he said earlier. It would be *contrary to public policy* to allow identical claims to be repeatedly litigated.

Estoppel cannot be used to authorise illegality. Thus, if powers that are *ultra vires* are assumed by a person or body, estoppel cannot be used to authorise what has been done (*Ministry of Agriculture and Fisheries v Matthews* (1950)).

Estoppel may apply where the act or statement is that of someone who is a 'privy' of one of the parties to the litigation in question. A 'privy' is someone who has a special type of legal connection to someone else, for example, for some purposes an agent is the privy of his principal, and vice versa.

For the purposes of evidence law, estoppel can be divided into three types:

- estoppel by previous judicial proceedings;
- estoppel by deed;
- estoppel by representation.

Estoppel by previous judicial proceedings

A judgment is conclusive against everyone in relation to the legal state of affairs that it produces. This is of special importance where the judgment affects the status of a person or thing (a 'judgment *in rem*'), for example, a judgment to the effect that a person is divorced, or that a ship seized in wartime is not a neutral vessel.

A judgment also has the effect of preventing the parties to an action, or their privies, from *denying the facts on which it is based*. This form of estoppel may operate either as 'cause of action estoppel' or as 'issue estoppel' and is based on two policy considerations:

● litigation should be final;

● nobody should be harassed twice in respect of the same cause of action.

See *Carl Zeiss Stiftung v Rayner and Keeler Ltd (No 2)* (1967).

Cause of action estoppel

Cause of action estoppel applies only when the cause of action in the earlier proceedings is identical to that in the later proceedings (*Buehler AG v Chronos Richardson Ltd* (1998)). It prevents a party to an action from asserting or denying, as against the other party, the existence of a particular cause of action, the existence of which has already been determined in a final judgment on the merits in previous litigation between the same parties. If judgment was given for the plaintiff in the earlier action, the cause of action no longer exists (and so cannot be sued on again) because the judgment has taken its place. If judgment was given for the defendant in the earlier action, the effect is that the earlier court has found the cause of action not to exist. As a result, the unsuccessful plaintiff can no longer assert that it does.

Originally, this form of estoppel was known as 'estoppel by record' (the record being that of the court delivering the judgment), but it is now immaterial whether the judicial decision has been pronounced by a tribunal that is required to keep a written record of its decisions or not (*Carl Zeiss Stiftung v Rayner and Keeler Ltd (No 2)* (1967)).

A final judgment 'on the merits' means a judgment on the cause of action that cannot be varied, re-opened or set aside by the court delivering it, or by any other court of equal jurisdiction, although it may be subject to appeal to a court of higher jurisdiction (*The Sennar (No 2) (1985)*).

There will be no judgment on the merits when an action is dismissed for want of prosecution (*In re Orrell Colliery and Fire-Brick Co* (1879)). Default judgments and judgments by consent are treated as judgments 'on the merits' (*Kok Hoong v Leong Cheong Kweng Mines Ltd* (1964)).

A judgment obtained by fraud or collusion will not give rise to an estoppel (*Duchess of Kingston's case* (1776)).

Issue estoppel

Issue estoppel can arise in circumstances where the causes of action are not the same. There are many causes of action that can be established only by proving that two or more different conditions are fulfilled. Such causes of action involve as many separate issues between the parties as there are conditions to be fulfilled by the plaintiff in order to establish his cause of action. If, in litigation on one cause of action, any of the separate issues as to whether a particular condition has been fulfilled is determined by a court of competent jurisdiction, neither party can, in subsequent litigation between one another on any cause of action that depends on the fulfilment of the identical condition, assert that the condition was fulfilled if the court in the first action determined that it was not. Nor can either party subsequently deny that such a condition was fulfilled if the court in the first action determined that it was (*Thoday v Thoday* (1964)).

For issue estoppel to apply, three conditions must be satisfied:

- the same issue must have been decided in the earlier case;

- the judicial decision in the earlier case must have been final;

- the parties to the decision, or their privies, must be the same persons as the parties to the proceedings in which the estoppel is raised, or their privies.

See *Carl Zeiss Stiftung v Rayner and Keeler Ltd (No 2) (1967)*.

Issue estoppel, like cause of action estoppel, is a feature of adversarial procedure. Where proceedings have an inquisitorial element, therefore, issue estoppel will not be strictly applied. So, for example, issue estoppel could rarely, if ever, apply to proceedings for divorce or to children's cases (*Re B (1997)*).

Under the rule in *Henderson v Henderson (1843)*, and in line with the decision of the House of Lords in *Johnson v Gore Wood (2000)*, issue estoppel has been extended to cover not only the case where a particular point has been raised and specifically determined in the earlier proceedings, but also the case where a party later attempts to raise a point that might have been, but was not, raised in the earlier proceedings. This is founded on the principle of public policy in preventing multiplicity of actions (*Talbot v Berkshire CC (1994)*).

However, for the rule in *Henderson v Henderson* to apply, the parties to the earlier decision must not only have been the same persons as the parties to the later action in which the estoppel is raised; they must also be suing or being sued in the later action in the *same capacities* as in the first (*Marginson v Blackburn BC (1939)*; *C (A Minor) v Hackney LBC (1996)*).

Where the first judgment was obtained by default, the rule in *Henderson v Henderson* is unlikely to be applied (*Arnold v National Westminster Bank plc (1991)*).

It may be that the rule in *Henderson* will in future be less strictly applied. In *Sweetman v Shepherd and Others (2000)*, the Court of Appeal held that the rule should not prevent a defendant from bringing a later action for an indemnity or contribution, even though he could have claimed the same relief in earlier proceedings in which he was sued with a codefendant.

Discovery of new evidence

The general rule is that a party who has been unsuccessful in litigation will not be allowed to re-open that litigation unless the new evidence entirely changes an aspect of the case, and it could not by reasonable diligence have been discovered before (*Phosphate Sewage Co Ltd v Molleson* (1879)). In *Arnold v National Westminster Bank plc*, Lord Keith suggested that it should be easier to overcome an issue estoppel than a cause of action estoppel where a party relies on further relevant material which he could not by reasonable diligence have adduced in the earlier proceedings.

Analogous provisions in criminal proceedings

In criminal law, the pleas of *autrefois acquit* and *autrefois convict* are available to prevent a defendant being put in what is sometimes called 'double jeopardy'. In *Connelly v DPP* (1964), Lord Morris laid down these propositions:

- a man cannot be tried for a crime in respect of which he has previously been acquitted or convicted;

- a man cannot be tried for a crime in respect of which he could on some previous indictment have been convicted;

- the same rule applies if the crime in respect of which he is being charged is in effect the same, or substantially the same, as a crime in respect of which he has been acquitted, or could have been convicted, or has been convicted;

- one test as to whether the rule applies is whether the evidence that is necessary to support the second indictment, or whether the facts that constitute the second offence, would have been sufficient to procure a conviction on the first indictment, either in relation to the offence charged or in relation to an offence of which, on that indictment, the accused could have been found guilty.

A substantial inroad into the common law has been made by
ss 54–57 of the Criminal Procedure and Investigations Act 1996.
These sections introduce the concept of 'tainted acquittals' and
apply to acquittals in respect of offences alleged to have been
committed on or after 15 April 1997.

The provisions apply where: (a) a person has been acquitted of
an offence; and (b) a person has been convicted of an
'administration of justice offence' involving interference with or
intimidation of a juror or a witness, or potential witness, in any
proceedings that led to the acquittal (s 54(1)).

Where it appears to the court before which the person was
convicted that there is a real possibility that, but for the
interference or intimidation, the acquitted person would not
have been acquitted, the court shall certify that it so appears,
unless it would be contrary to the interests of justice to take
proceedings against the acquitted person for the offence of
which he was acquitted, whether because of lapse of time or for
any other reason (s 54(2) and (5)).

Where a court has certified under these provisions, an
application may be made to the High Court for an order
quashing the acquittal. Where such an order is made,
proceedings may be taken against the acquitted person for the
offence in respect of which he was acquitted.

By s 55, the High Court shall not make an order quashing an
acquittal unless four conditions are satisfied:

- it appears to the High Court to be likely that, but for the
  interference or intimidation, the acquitted person would not
  have been acquitted;

- it does not appear to the court that, because of lapse
  of time, or for any other reason, it would be contrary
  to the interests of justice to take proceedings against
  the acquitted person for the offence of which he was
  acquitted;

- it appears to the court that the acquitted person has been given a reasonable opportunity to make written representations to the court;

- it appears to the court that the conviction for the administration of justice offence will stand. In determining whether this condition is satisfied, the court shall take into account all the information before it, but shall ignore the possibility of new factors coming to light.

There is no equivalent of issue estoppel in criminal proceedings (*DPP v Humphrys* (1977)).

Retrial for serious offences under the Criminal Justice Act 2003

Under s 75(1), a person may be retried for a qualifying offence of which he has been acquitted either on indictment in England and Wales, on appeal against conviction, verdict or finding in proceedings on indictment in England and Wales, or on appeal from a decision on such an appeal.

Qualifying offence

This is one that is identified in Part 1 of Sched 5 to the Act and includes such offences as murder, manslaughter, kidnapping, rape, intercourse with a girl under 13, Class A drug offences, arson endangering life, war crimes and acts of terrorism.

Application to the Court of Appeal

Section 76(1) provides that a prosecutor may apply to the Court of Appeal for an order quashing a person's acquittal and ordering him to be retried for the qualifying offence (*Re D (acquitted person: retrial)* (2006)).

Persons acquitted elsewhere other than in the United Kingdom

Section 76(2) further provides that a prosecutor may apply to the Court of Appeal to determine whether such an acquittal is a bar to the person being tried in England and Wales. In cases where there is found to be a bar, the prosecutor may then apply for an order that the acquittal should *not* be a bar.

Other offences related to the main offence

This provision will also relate to *any other* qualifying offence which the defendant could have been convicted of at the same time (the offence having appeared on the indictment). This will *exclude* an offence of which he has been convicted and an offence of which he has been found not guilty by reason of insanity. It will also exclude any offence where it was found that he did not do the act or make the omission having been found to be under a disability (as defined by s 4 of the Criminal Procedure (Insanity) Act 1964 (c 84)).

Consent of the Director of Public Prosecutions

Section 76(3) provides that the above applications can only be made with the consent of the Director of Public Prosecutions (DPP). The DPP may give his consent *only* if he is satisfied that:

(a) there is evidence as respects which the requirements of s 78 appear to be met;

(b) it is in the public interest for the application to proceed; and

(c) any trial pursuant to an order on the application would not be inconsistent with obligations of the United Kingdom under Art 31 or 34 of the Treaty on European Union relating to the principle of *ne bis in idem* s 76(4).

(See s 76(4).)

Section 78: new and compelling evidence

For a retrial to be ordered, there needs be new (not adduced in the earlier proceedings) and compelling evidence against the acquitted person in relation to the qualifying offence. Evidence is compelling if it is reliable, substantial and in the context of the outstanding issues, it appears highly probative of the case against the acquitted person.

Determination by the Court of Appeal

Section 77 provides that if the Court of Appeal is satisfied that the requirements of ss 78 and 79 are met, they *must* make the order applied for or, otherwise, must dismiss the application.

Section 79: interests of justice

Section 79(1) provides that it needs to be in the interests of justice for the court to order a retrial.

Under s 79(2), the court needs to have regard to:

(a) whether existing circumstances make a fair trial unlikely;

(b) for the purposes of that question and otherwise, the length of time since the qualifying offence was allegedly committed;

(c) whether it is likely that the new evidence would have been adduced in the earlier proceedings against the acquitted person but for a failure by an officer or by a prosecutor to act with due diligence or expedition;

(d) whether, since those proceedings or, if later, since the commencement of this Part, any officer or prosecutor has failed to act with due diligence or expedition.

Appeals

Section 33(1B) of the Criminal Appeal Act 1968 (as amended by s 81 of the Criminal Justice Act 2003) provides that either party, whether they are the acquitted person or prosecutor, may appeal to the House of Lords regarding any decision of the Court of Appeal on an application under s 76(1) or (2) of the Criminal Justice Act 2003.

Estoppel by deed

Where an action is brought on a deed, the parties to the deed and those claiming through them, such as successors in title, are estopped from denying the truth of the facts stated in the deed (*Bowman v Taylor* (1834)).

Whether recitals in a deed bind all the parties is a matter of construction in each case (*Greer v Kettle* (1938)).

Estoppel by deed will not operate so as to prevent a party from relying on fraud, duress, illegality, or any other fact entitling him to rescission or rectification of the deed (*Greer v Kettle* (1938)).

Estoppel by conduct

An estoppel may arise where it would be unconscionable for a person to deny a representation of fact that is implicit in his conduct. Such an estoppel may arise from:

● agreement;

● express or implied representation;

● negligence.

For there to be estoppel by conduct, the representation must relate to an existing fact and be unambiguous.

Agreement

A person may not deny the title to land of someone to whom he has paid rent for that land (*Cooke v Loxley* (1792)); nor may bailees, licensees and agents deny the title of their bailors, licensors or principals after having effectively acknowledged them in the transactions carried out on their behalf (*Gosling v Birnie* (1831); *Crossley v Dixon* (1863)).

Express or implied representation

Where a person, by words or conduct, wilfully causes another to believe in a certain state of things, and thereby induces him to act or to alter his own previous position, the representor will be estopped from alleging that a different state of affairs existed at the time when the representation was made (*Pickard v Sears* (1837); *Greenwood v Martins Bank Ltd* (1933)).

Negligence

To establish estoppel by negligence, it has to be proved that a duty of care was owed to the person who has suffered loss and that there has been a breach of that duty (*Coventry, Sheppard and Co v Great Eastern Rly* (1883); *Mercantile Bank of India Ltd v Central Bank of India Ltd* (1938)).